THE WESTERN REGION BOY SCOUTS OF AMERICA
WOULD LIKE TO THANK
ROBERT & CHERRY ANN SUTHERLAND
OF HAWAII FOR THEIR GENEROUS
PROVISION OF THIS BOOK.

IT IS THEIR HOPE THAT FAMILIES ACROSS AMERICA
WILL BENEFIT FROM THE ¡FAMILY FIRST¡ MESSAGE
BEATING THE MIDAS CURSE CONVEYS.

IN THE SPIRIT OF VALUES BEFORE VALUABLES,
THE SUTHERLANDS ARE PLEASED TO SHARE
THIS POWERFUL MESSAGE WITH ALL READERS.

Beating the Midas Cur$e

by

Perry L. Cochell and Rodney C. Zeeb

HERITAGE INSTITUTE PRESS, INC.
West Linn, Oregon

First Printing November 2005

ISBN 1-933694-00-9

Senior Project Editor: Brad Haga

Associate Editor: Robert Breyer

Cover Design: Nicole M. Lawry

Set in Warnock Pro Light

Printed and bound in the USA by Bridgetown Press Portland, Oregon

Heritage Institute Press, LLC
Willamette 205 Corporate Center
1800 Blankenship Road, Suite 310
West Linn, Oregon 97068
1-877-447-1659
www.beatingthemidascurse.com

Beating the Midas Cur$e

ACKNOWLEDGEMENTS

We would like to thank The Heritage Institute staff for all of their help with this endeavor. Thank you to Susan Wise, Ryan Zeeb, and Brian Bell for their input; to Mary Fieweger for her energy and thoughtfulness; to Camille Gould for her help with the research and bibliography; and to Nicole Lawry for her help in illustrating The Heritage Process™. We also want to thank the contributing authors for their help and insights and all of the rest of the members of The Heritage Institute for their support. And, special thanks to Richard and Sibylle Beck, G.M. "Milt" and Marilyn Butler, and Dave and Marcia Lantz for helping to make The Heritage Institute possible.

Perry

My special thanks to the Boy Scouts of America, who introduced me to the principles of guided discovery learning; to Roy Williams, Chief Scout Executive of the Boys Scouts of America, who has served as both a mentor and a friend; to the Scout Executives of the Western Region of the Boy Scouts of American who introduced me to their wonderful volunteers; to Everett Sumner who has taught me "that you can never communicate enough;" and, to Robert H. Cochran, a dear friend, for his pure example of a values-centered life.

On a more personal side, I thank my deceased father-in-law, Reed C. Hawkins, who taught me that "money is only as good as what it will do for you." I also thank my children, Parker, Camille, Laura, Rachel and Tanner for helping me pass along my values.

Most importantly, I thank my wife, Karen, for her genuineness as a caring person, her devotion to and love for me, and for our sacred companionship. I value her most.

Rod

My special thanks to Robert Esperti, who introduced me to the concepts of values-based planning and mentored me over the years; to my brother, Rick Zeeb, who helped me meld the principles of legacy planning with current financial planning; to Monica Estabrooke, with the AARP Foundation, for her passion for philanthropy and her insights into integrating these principles with charities; to Susan Wise, who helped me work with so many families since 1989; and to the many attorneys, CPAs, financial advisors and non-profits who have allowed me to work with their clients and donors.

And, a very special thank you to my children, Christina and Ryan, who have helped me focus my values and have provided pure joy in my life.

Perry and Rod

Our gratitude is endless to the clients, friends and others who have trusted us with assisting them in passing on their values to future generations.

Finally, both Perry and Rod thank Brad Haga for his encouragement and support with this book. We would not have taken on this project without his encouragement and expertise.

TABLE OF CONTENTS

FOREWORD

The architect came to the law office with an urgent request. His father had a terminal illness and at best a few years to live. He had built an estate worth over twelve million dollars but had not completed his estate planning. As with many people, that procrastination changed the minute the doctor gave him the 'long' face. The architect said that his father and mother knew exactly how they wanted their estate to be distributed. They had five children, three daughters and two sons (including the architect) plus eighteen grandchildren. The sons were financially independent. For the daughters, it had been a rocky road; each was divorced, and they had all gone through tough financial times.

To help them out, the parents had recently purchased homes for their daughters, paid in full. Plus, to make sure their daughters and grandchildren would be taken care of, the parents wanted a significant amount of their wealth transferred to the girls when they passed on. For the sons, the parents instructed that trusts be created that would be accessible when they retired. Finally, the architect said his parents were in a hurry to have their wishes translated into all of the necessary estate documents as quickly as possible.

The elderly couple's wishes were clear. There were no complex legal or financial structures in place that would slow the process, so their estate planning documents came together quickly. Instruments were developed to transfer a significant amount of money to the daughters, and tax-favorable trusts were created that would be paid to the sons in the future. From a purely legal and financial standpoint, this estate plan was well-thought out, carefully crafted, and complied with the highest national standards. It was, in fact, a textbook application of the best traditional estate planning that was available then—or even now, for that matter.

But as the poet Robert Burns reminds us, "The best laid plans of mice and men often go awry..."

One week to the day after the planning was complete, the architect called with news of a death in the family. However, it was his mother, not his father, who had unexpectedly died. And there was more: six days after her death, his grieving father passed away. This estate plan had come full circle, from planning to implementation, in just a few weeks.

As planned, the estate's assets were subjected to minimal taxation. The money the parents wanted to make available immediately for the daughters was transferred to them, and the trusts established for future distribution to the sons were in place.

To be honest, there was no small amount of satisfaction (OK, pride!) on the part of the author of the plan; everything that could be done to help this family minimize taxes and to pass the wealth to the children had been done—and in record time. This was what being an estate planning attorney was all about.

Two years later, the architect returned to the office. His story of what had happened to the family after the distribution of his parent's assets was heartbreaking. They were being torn apart. His three sisters were in deep financial trouble. Each had spent her share of the inheritance. Every penny. All three homes, gifts from the parents, had been mortgaged to the hilt.

Now, the architect said, the sisters were demanding that he and his brother tap their own inheritance trusts to help them, because it was "what mom and dad would want them to do." But how could he? He knew that any money they were given would quickly evaporate. Their spending has always been out of control, he said. What happened, he wanted to know? What could he do? How could he bring his family back together?

The best laid plans, indeed.

This family was in chaos, and there wasn't a legal solution in the book that could glue them back together. It took less than twenty-four months for the daughters to spend most of the assets the parents had worked for fifty years to build. Worst of all, the family unity that all parents wish for their children was devastated. In a very real sense, all of that money, and all of those carefully crafted asset transfer plans and tax reduction strategies, had been rendered meaningless.

And yet, it was not the planning that had failed. It accomplished exactly what it was designed to do: transfer the greatest amount of assets with the smallest tax liability possible to the heirs. By any generally accepted legal or financial standard, by any purely objective definition of a 'successful' plan, this one was a gold plated winner.

The operation, to coin a phrase, was a complete success. (Pity the patient died, of course.)

Can you envision any scenario in which these parents (or any parents!) would have hoped that this would be their final legacy? A broken family? A squandered fortune?

In our years of combined experience and research, we have seen too many good plans disintegrate the moment the assets began to flow through the fingers of unprepared heirs. We have worked with thousands of families, from the moderately wealthy to some of the richest in America. What have we seen? Children who did not understand what it took for their parents to accumulate their wealth, and who were never taught a proper relationship with money. Children who were not aware that their family's wealth, like most affluent people's, consisted of just two things: real estate and securities—not cash. ("OK, but show me the real money," are the most common words attorneys hear during the estate settlement process.)

We have seen families ripped to shreds as they battle over money. And (most tragically from our perspectives not just as attorneys, but as parents ourselves), we have seen too many children who never learned that the most important inheritance their parents left to them had nothing whatsoever to do with money.

Nor, as you will see, is this kind of destruction and chaos the exception to the rule in estate planning. Ask any advisor who works within the estate planning arena how often they see families thrown into turmoil and fortunes lost because the money—not the family—was the focus of the planning. Be prepared to hold onto your hat when they answer. (Which we will do ourselves shortly.)

We came to the conclusion that families are not adequately served by a traditional estate planning system that suggests that the transfer of assets and the promotion of tax savings are the most important legacy that one generation should strive to pass to the next. That is not, by any means, a criticism of the advisors who construct traditional plans. They do their jobs (which to be honest we should call 'death planning,' not estate planning) well, within the confines of the planning products they are charged to construct. The responsibility of the traditional advisor is to transfer assets and to reduce taxes, not to save families.

This book, and the process of planning it describes, was born out of the needs we saw in people like the architect in this story--needs that existing legal and financial providers could not answer. Our experiences led us to two major conclusions about money and families:

- We believe that the tide of family destruction caused by money can be resolved and its effects reversed.

- We believe that traditional planning advisors can work as partners with what we call *The Heritage Process* to construct living plans that can strengthen the family across generations in ways no will, trust, or bank account can ever do.

The Heritage Process has been two decades in development, but, as you will see, it represents one of the most significant shifts in thinking in the field of financial and estate planning since the sixteenth century. Thousands of families have already experienced the 'family first, fortune second' perspective of this Process. They have learned that by putting their values ahead of their valuables as they plan, they greatly increase the chances of securing both of them--for their children and their children's children, for generations to come.

Finally, this note: the underlying premise of the Heritage Process, that the values you live by are your most important asset, and the greatest inheritance your children will receive, has nothing to do with affluence.

It's not about the money. It's about your family.

Perry L. Cochell   Rodney C. Zeeb

West Linn, Oregon
October 2005

Introduction

Imagine a world where there was a ninety percent probability that you'd take a tumble the minute you got out of bed. Then, a nine out of ten chance that there would be no hot water when you stepped into the shower. Followed by the same degree of certainty that your spouse would say, "Sorry honey, no food in the fridge, you'll have to grab something on the way to the office."

Which by the way, would be pretty unlikely given the overwhelming odds your car wouldn't start when you turned the ignition. Maybe not such a bad thing, either, since those pesky nine out of ten odds would follow you out the driveway and make you a shoo-in to be involved in a car accident once you finally got on the road. As for your chances of walking away from that one…. in our ninety percent world, Las Vegas won't be taking any bets on your going dancing this weekend.

A ninety percent probability of *anything* happening makes that event, by scientific standards, an actuarial certainty.

Fortunately, in the real world, our chances of having to stare doom in the face on a daily basis are pretty limited. The odds of being struck by lightning sometime in your life are still 1 in 3,000, of being attacked by a shark, about 1 in 700,000.

Those are odds we can—and do—live with. It goes against human nature to suggest that any of us would set out to get married, build a house, start a business, have children or do anything else important knowing there was a ninety percent chance that we'd fail.

Consider, however, estate planning. If there is one area of your life where you really want to hit the bulls-eye, it's here. Of course, we try to share our dreams, our hopes, and our most important values with those we love while we are alive, but we also have an instinctive desire to provide for our families after we're gone. We want to leave a legacy that provides meaning, not just money. Plus, we want to know that our lives meant something, that in our passage through this world we made a difference.

Psychologists say it is not death we fear so much. It is insignificance. The idea that, at the end of the day, our lives didn't amount to all that much. That we didn't set ripples in motion in the lives of our families, friends and neighbors that would carry our accomplishments and our values on for generations.

The human desire to leave a significant legacy is extremely powerful. Across the centuries people have expended enormous energy and resources to develop mechanisms by which they could protect and pass on their valuables to their heirs. Whether the estate is that of a pauper or a prince, the driving force behind estate planning has always been to provide for the future, to ensure that your loved ones will have basic necessities like homes, medical care, and education.

Each of us will leave a legacy of some sort, whether we plan for it or not, whether we have children or not. The poet and the artist leave ideas and images to future generations. Working people may leave a home, and some insurance. The self-employed businessman may leave factories, investment portfolios, and complex trusts. No matter what you have accomplished in life, or how much or how little you have accumulated, one thing is certain:

Whether by choice or by chance, you will leave something behind.

Now, the bad news. The overwhelming odds are that what you really wanted to leave your family probably won't be anything like what they will actually receive. They will not benefit from what you hoped for them, or what you planned for with your will and other legal documents. That's because, as we have learned though our own research and experience, in nine out of ten cases, the things your family truly needs to thrive and prosper across the years won't even be discussed during your estate planning process.

Why not? Because there really is an upside-down world, where a ninety percent failure rate is the norm. It has existed for years. And, dominated by the combined forces of inertia and tradition, it continues to this day. It has been the reality of the world of financial and estate planning for centuries. It is accepted without question from the boardrooms of Fortune 500 companies to the ivory towers of academia. Because of it, relationships will be broken, families destroyed, businesses devastated, and fortunes lost.

6

Ask an auditorium filled with financial planners and estate planning attorneys if this world exists and you'll see every head nod in agreement.

We have worked with thousands of families over the past two decades. Through that experience, from our research of the financial and legal literature, and from interviews and interactions with professional colleagues in several disciplines, we have come to this conclusion:

Ninety percent of all traditional inheritance plans will fail.

In part, this conclusion is based on numerous studies that show in families where new wealth has been created by the first generation, six out of ten of those families' fortunes will be gone by the end of the second generation. By the end of the third generation, nine out of the ten families will be broke.

This book is born out of that conclusion. It is why The Heritage Institute was founded, and it was the engine behind the development of a unique tool (called The Heritage Process) designed to combat the ninety percent failure rate. As we write this introduction, this process has already been experienced by thousands of people. Now, we'd like to share it with you.

This book is founded on a simple premise: we believe that when parents who build wealth pass only their *material assets* to their children, and not the values by which they have lived, there is little chance the family, or its wealth, will survive for long.

That is not to say that we dismiss the products or process of traditional estate planning outright; on the contrary, investments, trusts and other financial and legal instruments are, and always will be, the vehicle for the transmission of the *things* a family owns. But money is just a tool, as likely to separate families as it is to unify them. Your financial net worth is a statistic, not a legacy. To appreciate that fact is to understand that your family cannot be defined in terms of the things you *own*; real estate valuations, spreadsheets, trust documents and bank account balances describe a *condition*, not a family. You and your children, your grandchildren and generations of your family yet unborn, can only be defined by the values, the traditions, the faith and the ethics which have shaped your unique family history for many years.

What, then, is a legacy by the terms of our definition? If material assets are not the most important things we leave behind, what is? Also, how do we go about shaping such a 'non-material' legacy and communicating it to those we love? These questions have been the focus of our research and work for many years.

We have learned that when families place their *valuables* ahead of their *values,* they will end up with neither. We believe that the most important inheritance your children will receive from you comes while you are still alive. It is embedded in your everyday life. It is made up of the values you learned from important people in your own life. This is an inheritance you live and model to your family, friends, co-workers, and the community of people and organizations who make up your world.

In short, we are dedicated to seeing that more families don't become part of "the ninety percent."

If your priorities during life are your family and your values, you should maintain those priorities with death (estate) planning. That means making sure that the financial inheritance you leave will be regarded as a tool and a resource to support the real inheritance of values your children have already received.

The traditional estate planning process that has been the norm for centuries* has focused on money (get more) and taxes (pay less), rather than on family and values (at all).   But, as we noted, ninety percent of the time traditional planning fails in its primary mission of keeping the money in the family.

The Heritage Process helps people put their family before their fortune as they plan. In doing so, the chances that the family can thrive in its relationships and still prosper materially for generations are greatly enhanced. Families who go through the Process come to a better understanding of their relationship to wealth, and with one another. They learn to communicate more clearly and more honestly about things like money, philanthropy, as well as about their shared goals and objectives. They learn–by doing, not just by talking–how to make the money a tool to achieve the most important goals of all–family unity and individual achievement. They listen to stories about the hardships and triumphs that brought the family to where it is today, and they talk openly and from the heart about deeply important matters, like the sustaining quality of faith.

---

* For more information on how estate planning has developed over the ages, please see Appendix 1, *A Brief History of Estate Planning*

The following chapters will show how contemporary estate planning systems evolved, and explain how traditional planning, when done from a tax minimizing and asset enhancement perspective only, often achieves the opposite results it intended to accomplish. You'll learn how any family, from average middle-class income earners to the 'super-rich,' can be torn apart by '*affluenza*,' a dysfunctional relationship with wealth. You'll see how families just like yours use philanthropy and other tools to turn the problems of affluenza into opportunities that benefit important causes in which the family believes, while strengthening the family itself.

Plus, we'll show how grandparents can play an important role as mentors to their grandkids, and why, even though it's great to start early, it is never too late to begin mentoring children and grandchildren. The Heritage Process is for all families—not just the affluent. Its guiding rules and principles just make sense. It does not adhere to a rigid set of hard and fast rules; it is built on general principles that anyone can understand.

We believe that traditional planning has failed too many families. We have learned that the tools you need to strengthen and unify your family across generations are already in your possession. With those tools, you can begin to turn the ninety percent world on its head.

You *can* pass both your values and your valuables to your children.

Perry L. Cochell and Rodney C. Zeeb met in law school longer ago than either wants to admit. For the past twenty-plus years, they have worked separately and together with families of all types and values. After law school, Perry and Rod began their legal careers in separate private practices. In 1994, Perry began working with the Boy Scouts and has been one of the top charitable giving advisors in the nation for many years. Rod remained in private practice and is one of the nation's top legal advisors specializing in the fields of financial, charitable, and estate planning for affluent clients. They were fully aware of "the ninety percent world," but instead of wondering what to do about it, they took action.

Working independently and together, Perry and Rod each developed their concept of values-based planning. Together, they formed The Heritage

Institute. Refining and perfecting what came to be known as The Heritage Process, Rod and Perry set out to share their proprietary system with other professionals. Heritage advisors, members of The Heritage Institute, have had extensive training and education in all aspects of The Heritage Process. Most have earned, or are in the process of earning, a CWC designation as a Certified Wealth Consultant–meaning they have completed a comprehensive series of courses in the field of values-based legacy planning that has been compared to a Masters Degree. (See Appendix for requirements.)

This book examines how modern estate planning came to be, and how true values-based planning asks the questions and seeks the answers to the questions that really concern people as they plan for the future of their families. It also represents Perry and Rod's desire to inform people about the potential enhancements that can be made to traditional estate planning through the benefits of The Heritage Process.

The Story of King Midas

Some people who pick this book up for the first time will rack their brain to recall the story of King Midas, whose mythical affliction was the inspiration for our title.

You may recall the ancient Greek legend...

Midas was known to be a kind man, blessed with financial abundance. He had a beautiful palace with extensive gardens in which he loved to walk. He loved animals and kept favorite pets. The apple of his eye was his beautiful daughter; just hearing her laugh brought him joy. And he had a tremendous amount of wealth, mostly in bars and bags of gold.

Midas loved gold. He would go into his royal treasury and gaze at it for hours on end. He loved the way it shone, the noise it made when he would throw coins up in the air and let them shower down over his head. He liked the smoothness of it in his hand. He loved to earn it, count it and hoard it. Midas was a happy man.

One day he came upon old Silenus, a friend of the god Dionysus, wandering lost in the forest. Midas took Silenus home and cared for him for eleven days. When Dionysus finally found his friend, he was so grateful for Midas's kindness that he granted him one wish. Against the advice of the god, Midas asked that everything he touch turn to gold.

When he woke the next morning, he tentatively touched the table next to his bed. It instantly turned to gold. Midas leaped up, and laughing and dancing began touching every-thing in sight: the floors, the walls, the draperies, the furniture. He ran through the palace grounds touching tables, statues, paintings, trees, and even the palace gates.

He was delirious with joy! In one instant, all of his dreams had come true. Piles of pure gold, glorious and perfect, sent from heaven—and it was all his with only a simple, effortless touch! No work, no sacrifice, no planning. He had realized his deepest desire. He was rich, rich beyond calculation, and there was no end to how much he could possess. Surely, he was the most blessed of men.

Out of breath, he stopped to walk through his beloved garden and picked a rose to smell. By the time he brought it to his nose, it was lifeless metal. Midas paused. He would have to be careful from now on and just bend over a flower to sniff it. Exhausted and hungry, he decided to have a meal. But by the time he put a grape in his mouth it had turned hard and cold. He nearly choked on wine that turned to liquid gold in his throat.

His favorite cat jumped onto his lap and suddenly, instead of the soft fur he loved, there was only a cold statue. Midas began to cry in despair as he realized what he had done. His beloved daughter, hearing his distress, ran to comfort him with a hug; and before he could stop her she, too, was transformed. Midas was heartbroken. Truly repentant now, he begged Dionysus to take away his curse. Knowing that he had learned his lesson, Dionysus told Midas what he must do.

"First, you must wash your hands in the river. Then bring jugs of water from the river, and pour them over the things you changed. Second, you must give away all of your wealth."

Midas promised. He followed the god's instructions and soon his beautiful daughter was restored to him. Hearing her laugh again brought him to tears. King Midas gave all of his wealth to the poor, and moved to a small cabin in the woods, where he and his beloved daughter lived out their days in complete happiness.

The story of King Midas is not just a cautionary tale about greed, or a warning to be careful for what you wish. It is an enduring reminder of the things in life from which true happiness springs. Traditional estate planning with its assets-only focus, misses those things. Wills, trusts, stocks, real estate deeds–even money itself–are just pieces of paper. King Midas discovered that real happiness could be achieved only if he put love for family before love for fortune.

This book is dedicated to that ideal.

Family first

PART I

CHAPTER ONE

The Fire

The October night is clear and cool. Smoke drifts from a few chimneys in the wooded neighborhood, thinning to whispers before disappearing against the face of the full moon. Piles of orange and brown leaves dot the streets, each neatly-raked mound a testament to the ritual that pulls families away from football games and indoor chores on autumn weekends.

At the end of a cul-de-sac, sits a two-story Cape Cod framed by a big leaf maple and a towering fir. A well-worn basketball hoop is mounted above the garage, and two Malibu-Barbie bikes lean against a covered woodshed that's piled high with cords of seasoned oak and apple wood.

Then, from the back yard, a single, half-hearted bark as Max lifts his head from between his paws and peers from the warmth of his shelter to warn away a pilfering squirrel who races to safety behind a bush next to the daylight basement window. Work and school and errands are just a few hours off; right now, Max and the rest of the world are at rest.

The squirrel is also ready for sleep, but a sudden burst of light from the basement window sends it skittering across the yard, up the fence and into the dependable safety of the maple tree. Then all of the basement windows fill with light, as a pile of varnish-soaked rags ignites next to the old water heater. Flames gnaw at the top of the antique library table Jack was re-finishing, then jump to a nearby shelf with its open tin cans of turpentine and shellac.

The fire begins to feel its strength, and twists and flings its fingers upward in search of fuel. It feeds on everything: paint cans, old books and folded cotton clothing. Then, it curls up around the stairs, and, with a ferocious surge, to the exposed joists in the basement ceiling. The basement is engulfed in moments, and as smoke begins to fan up into the house through the furnace vents, the hallway smoke alarm comes to life.

Jack wakes first and shakes his wife from her deep sleep. As they leap from bed, they can already smell the thick, varnish-laden smoke. They realize they have to get the kids out right now. It only takes a moment to pull their frightened children from their beds, race down the stairs through the billowing smoke, out the front door and into the moonlit yard.

As Jack literally shoves his wife and children out the door, he can see flames appearing in the back rooms of the house. Heat and smoke gather with brutal intensity. He realizes if the fire is still in the back of the house, in the kitchen and back bath, he has time to go back inside. Only a minute, maybe forty or fifty seconds, but still, time to grab something. Time to get a few important things before the fire destroys everything his family owns.

But...what? What should he take? He hesitates in the entryway. His briefcase and laptop computer are down the hallway in his home office. Easy to get to. Important, too, especially since much of his original research data and notes haven't been backed up. There'd be hell to pay at work if he set this project back by a couple of months.

He knows he has only a moment to decide what to grab, just what he and his family absolutely need. All that information...finances, business, taxes and insurance...a nightmare to have to rebuild.

The fire is roaring now, and the heat slams against him like a desert wind. He can hear sirens in the distance at the same instant that windows in the kitchen begin to pop and explode as the fire pushes relentlessly against the walls in search of more oxygen.

Jack starts down the hallway, coughing against the acrid smoke that rolls across the ceiling like gray ocean waves. The fire must have started in the basement, he thinks, the wooden floor is searing hot beneath his bare feet.

As he races towards the office door, he suddenly feels as if he is being watched. In a way he is. Five generations of family line the walls: from the 1847 tintypes of his wife's great-great grandparents, to WWII pictures of handsome young men in uniform, wedding and christening photos, picnics and family reunions.... the birth of his children. He only has a second to look, but in that instant he sees more than he's noticed in the thousands of trips he had made down the hall over the past ten years.

Ten years in this house. Ten years of walking through his family history every morning and every night. Why hasn't he made copies?

No time to worry about that now. The heat is fierce, and it is getting harder to see through the smoke. There is time to get one good arm load; he has to get out! The sirens are so loud now they sound like they are in his garage. That's good, he thinks, the fire department is here. His wife and kids will be fine.

He'll be OK, too. Just grab as much as he can. One load. He takes two more steps down the hall, and turns into his office. The room is bathed in a smoky, orange glow—just enough to see by.

What to take? There are the banker's boxes, bulging with years' worth of financial records. On the desk, his laptop screen glows softly, beckoning with files of data that had taken two months to research and develop. And in the filing cabinet, so many records, so much stuff....and then, he remembers the silver! His wife's silver plate and cutlery. Collecting heirloom silver is her passion, and a considerable investment, to boot. Will it survive the heat of the inferno if he leaves it in the house? Will they be able to find any of it in the ashes after the fire is extinguished? How hot does it have to get before silver melts....and how much can he carry, anyway?

Wait a minute. What about their personal financial records in the two bankers' boxes in the closet? Years' worth, and all critical for taxes and planning. Plus, his life insurance papers...Why hadn't he purchased a fire proof safe? He'd thought about it so many times. Where were they, oh yes, in a shoebox next to the filing cabinet. Weren't the trust deed documents in there, too, and all the rest of his bank records?

His kids' report cards and their birth certificates. Passports, too.

It had only been about fifteen seconds since he ran back into the house, but it seemed he'd been there an eternity. The heat is suffocating now, the smoke is thick, black and greasy. All right, time to decide. Take it, don't look back, and don't regret the choice. There was so much they would need, so many documents and records upon which they depended.

Then a crash, and sounds of wood splitting as the kitchen floor caves in, and a great whooshing noise as the blaze from the basement surges up into the house.

21

That was it. Jack makes his decision. He fills his arms until he can barely see over the load, and runs as fast as he can, down the smoky hallway, out onto the porch, and into the sweet, clear night air. His wife and children are under the maple tree, shivering in their pajamas. Max stands at attention in front of them; whatever is going on isn't going to get past him to hurt his family.

Several neighbors are already there comforting them. A police cruiser and two fire trucks race up to the curb, firefighters hit the ground and run towards the fully engulfed house before their trucks come to a complete stop.

Jack lurches towards his wife, the load in his arms about to fall. She sees him, and grateful tears well in her eyes; her family is safe. That's all that matters right now.

And then she sees what he has gathered in his arms, the things he risked his life to save as their home—everything they had accumulated—was burning down around him. She rushes to help him and embrace him, and her tears turn to deep sobs.

She takes as much as she can from his arms and then turns back to her children. She sees the fire hoses come to life and hears the urgency in the Chief's voice as he shouts to his men to attack the flames that crackle above the house, shooting thousands of glowing embers into the starry night.

She looks again at what her husband carried through the fire. The only things she has to begin building their new home.

And she smiles.

Now, your house is on fire

Your own home is burning, and, like Jack, your family is safely outside. You have less than a minute to grab something(s) of importance to you and your family.

Please think about these questions. If you're doing this with a spouse, friend or other family member, write your answers down privately and then compare them. Sharing your honest answers is half the fun, so, don't give them any hints.

1. What do you think Jack chose to carry out with him? Why did you come to that conclusion?

2. What would you take? Why?

3. Was it a tough decision?

4. Was your decision based on a personal value or on a sense of the financial or material importance of what you chose?

Now, share your answers with your spouse or other person with whom you're doing this. Did you make the same choices?

For the same reasons?

CHAPTER TWO

In Tradition We Trust?

*"Every object in a state of uniform motion tends to remain in that
state of motion unless an external force is applied to it."*
Sir Isaac Newton

The authors of this book regularly address groups of the men and women who plan for and manage the money of the most affluent Americans. They include estate planning attorneys, financial planners, CPAs and planned-giving officers for non-profits. These professionals are the best in their fields.   When they walk in the door for the first day of an intensive three-day course titled *Counseling the Affluent,* they bring with them years of practical, hands-on experience dealing with some of the nation's wealthiest families and individuals.

Their clients encompass every ethnic, religious and cultural background, with net worths ranging from a few million to several billion dollars (and change). Their backgrounds vary, from manufacturers and physicians, to real estate developers, Fortune 500 CEOs, athletes and actors, even the occasional "dot-commer" who got out while tech stocks were still worth something. No two of these advisors' clients are quite alike, and no two of their financial or estate plans will look the same.

But, as Perry Cochell and Rod Zeeb look out over the audience, they know there is at least one "tradition" that several client families of every advisor in the group have shared.

"Let me ask for a show of hands," Perry will say. *"How many of you have personally seen client families that have been destroyed in one way or another as a direct result of their affluence?"* Hands shoot up instantly. All of them. At every presentation.

"How many of you have seen an estate built by a client blown away by his or her children and grandchildren?" Again, raised hands fill the meeting room.

"Now," continues Rod, *"how many of you think the parents or grandparents who spent their lives building the family wealth planned for that to happen?"* For the first time, no hands are raised.

Around the room, the advisors to affluent families exchange knowing glances. They've seen the eighteen-year old get a million dollars cash, no strings attached, under the terms of grandad's will. Followed immediately by the hot car, the cocaine, the parties, and finally rehab, jail, or even suicide. They've seen marriages break up, friendships devastated, and family members alienated from each other. They've watched the companies that grandparents and parents sweated and sacrificed for decades to build go under, as heirs eager to squeeze more cash from the estate broke them up, sold them at bargain prices, or lost them through mismanagement.

From a legal, technical and 'state-of-the-art' traditional planning perspective, the advisors to the families going through these problems followed prudent, conservative and generally accepted standards and practices as they crafted their clients' financial and estate plans.

They diligently planned for the future of client valuables. They sought out every legal deduction, capitalized on the latest federal rulings relative to investments and trusts, and crafted complex instruments to minimize estate taxes.

They followed tradition. Sadly, so did many of the heirs.

The collapse of wealth over several generations is not news to your financial or legal advisors. It wasn't news two thousand years ago when a Chinese scholar penned the adage: *"fu bu guo san dai,"* or "Wealth never survives three generations." Or in thirteenth century England, where the proverb, *"Clogs to clogs in three generations,"* had morphed by the 1600s to *"Rags to riches to rags."* In nineteenth century America, where fortunes were made and lost with astounding speed amidst the gold fields, oil wells, copper mines and railroad booms, people said *"From shirtsleeves to shirtsleeves in three generations."*

Many cultures. Thousands of years of history. One common tradition of failure.

Adam Smith summed it up over two hundred years ago in his landmark book *The Wealth of Nations.* "Riches, in spite of the most violent regulations of law to prevent their dissipation, very seldom remain long in the same family."

How did these traditions evolve? And, why do we continue them? To get some perspective, let's take a trip to the bank.

The marble porticos, heroic statues and Georgian façade of the Bank of England's central office on Threadneedle Street in London are among the best known architectural features in the world. As you walk through the massive bronze entry and past the liveried doorman, you might get a sense that very little has changed since King William and Queen Mary created the bank in 1694. And you'd be right—in more ways than you might think.

The bank* was created because the public finances of England were weak, and the system of money and credit was in disarray. With a loan of a million pounds from one of the nation's wealthiest men, the new national bank was founded. In just a few short years, the practices and traditions of the Bank of England became a model for the world.

Today, customers can make deposits or withdrawals, open and manage checking accounts, apply for loans, purchase government-backed bonds, get investment portfolio advice, plan for retirement or meet with their private bank officer. One stop financial planning and money management.

Of course, in September, 1734, when the Bank of England moved into its present location, the very same menu of services was available to customers.

---

*The term BANK is derived from banco, the Italian word for bench, as the Lombard Jews in Italy kept benches in the market place where they exchanged money and bills. When a banker failed, his bench was broken up by the populace; and from this custom sprang the term "bankrupt." (Francis, History of the Bank of England, p.15)

Except for the ruffled clothing and powdered wigs, a customer from the year 2006 would find almost everything in the great institution of nearly three centuries ago to be very familiar.

The motto of bankers worldwide since the fourteenth century has been "Let the money do the work." It is a tradition they have followed scrupulously through wars and depressions, boom times and bust. What is extraordinary is that in their combined roles as repository, guardian and manager of our money, banks at the dawn of the twenty-first century are really so similar to those of five hundred years ago. Of course, they accomplish the movement of money and information at a much faster pace, and, sad but true, you were not given a toaster when you opened a savings account in the 1800s.

The banking industry has long occupied a central role in estate planning. For many people, banks are *the* key player in the process, as they perform vital trust management, investment guidance and other financial services relative to the establishment, maintenance, and ultimate disposition of estate assets.

If we were to travel back in time four thousand years to ancient Egypt to attend the public reading of a last will and testament, the proceedings would look a lot like they do today (well, except for the chariots outside the attorney's office). The products and services offered by the most modern banks to globe-trotting businessmen are nearly identical to what a wool merchant from the Scottish Highlands could find when he climbed out of a hansom cab at the steps of the Bank of England three hundred years ago. Sir Isaac Newton would call that inertia. We could just as easily call it tradition.

Tradition is a powerful concept. It reminds us of our duty to family, community, country and faith. It provides a framework for our routines and rituals, from weddings and funerals to our daily conduct of business. It provides important cultural and historical cohesion. However, when it comes to examining the role that tradition plays in financial planning, and in particular estate planning, there's a flip side of the tradition "coin" at which we should be looking.

That's the side that shows the *Titanic* ramming the iceberg. Icebergs were hardly unknown at the time. The ship's designers and engineers were certain that the *Titanic* was unsinkable. After all, they had planned it that way. Or, to stretch the analogy further, traditional planning is potentially hazardous because it only addresses the visible part of the iceberg—your money—and ignores all of what lies hidden beneath the surface: your hopes and dreams, your values, and especially, your family.

As Mark Twain noted, tradition should be our guide—not our jailer. Nowhere is that idea more important than in the way we *should* look at the institutions and practices that have guided estate planning for hundreds of years. From the perspective of professional advisors, money management has always tended to be a fairly conservative discipline. But for their clients, especially those who have inherited sizeable estates, that is not always the case. To see that fact demonstrated, you need only to attend a gathering of the men and women who plan for and manage the money of the most affluent Americans.

We are not suggesting that the mechanics of traditional financial and estate planning have not undergone tremendous change since William and Mary chartered the Bank of England. On the contrary, the increase in the variety and complexity of the tools, products and strategies available to advisors in the past twenty-five years alone is nothing short of breathtaking.

Further, the evolution of the world wide web, and its implications for the financial world has created more than a paradigm shift: it is *cataclysmic* in its implications for the future, at least from a transactional perspective. Many people feel that the immediacy and totality of information from the net is a major boon to financial planning.

The web certainly delivers in that department. (Scientists at the CERN particle physics laboratory in Switzerland recently sent a full-length DVD movie—*Star Wars*, what else?!—to colleagues at the California Institute of Technology in just under seven seconds, more than twenty thousand times faster than a typical home broadband connection.)

More information faster. Sophisticated analytical tools. Plus, of course, cool, user-friendly interfaces. All designed to complete more transactions at a greater speed and with higher efficiency than ever before in history.

We don't just live in an information age, we are awash in information. This deluge of facts, statistics and news may well be the most significant development in the history of human knowledge, with tremendous implications for each of us. So great is the impact that more and more contemporary scholars are saying that we may be witnessing the end of history as we have known it.

Consider:

The University of California, Berkeley, has a *"How Much Information"* project, which studies the amount of information produced each year. They point out that the world's total yearly production of print, film, optical, and magnetic content would require roughly 1.5 billion gigabytes of storage. This is the equivalent of two hundred fifty megabytes per person for each man, woman, and child on earth.

Of course, there is more...

- A single issue of the daily <u>New York Times</u> now contains more information than the seventeenth century man or woman would have encountered in a lifetime.

- A (possibly apocryphal) story tells that, at only twelve years of age, John Stuart Mill had read the entire amount of written information available in the world in English and French. Today, only a hundred and fifty years later, as we go from grade school to high school we learn only *one billionth* of what there is to learn. There is enough scientific information written every day to fill seven complete sets of the *Encyclopedia Britannica*; there is enough scientific information written every year to keep a person busy reading day and night for four hundred sixty years!

- Moore's Law (by Gordon Moore, co-founder of Intel) in computing says that information processing doubles in speed every 18 months.

- The sum total of human knowledge now doubles every two to three years. (Meaning that your personal knowledge must double every two to three years just to remain at your current level of ability, income and success in your chosen or current field of work.)
  And you might want to increase your vitamins: by the year 2020, it is expected that the sum total of human knowledge will double every *seventy-two days*.

- More than eighty percent of the world's technological knowledge has been developed in this century.

- About one thousand books are published internationally every day, and the total of all printed knowledge doubles every five years.

- Scientific information doubles every five years and scientific knowledge doubles every ten years.

- In the last thirty years mankind has produced more information than in the previous five thousand.

- In his book *Brain Longevity,* Dr. Dharma Singh Khalsa says the average American sees sixteen thousand advertisements, logos and labels in a day.

- The average Fortune 1000 worker already is sending and receiving approximately 178 messages and documents each day.

- Technology reduces the amount of time it takes to do any one task yet increases the number of tasks that people are expected to do (ie., answering your email). [1]

Clearly, as we plan for our financial lives, and for the things we want to leave to our inheritors, a lack of concrete information about plans and programs available to us isn't an issue. Information we have. Traditional programs to minimize taxes and shelter income, we have. Incredibly sophisticated software tools, that can analyze and assess hundreds of possible financial futures for us with the stroke of a key, we have.

What is missing, what has always been missing, is a broader context underlying the financial and estate plans we develop. A context based on historical reality, one that acknowledges and appreciates the role of the unique values that have shaped and guided your family for generations.

We want to be clear that within the framework of traditional financial planning are elements that are, and always will be, important. Ultimately, the numbers must be crunched, the assets allocated, the tax liability landscape surveyed.

However, traditional estate plans are manufactured in isolation. Accounting, actuarial and legal formulas are applied with 'one-size-fits-all' certainty. The estate continues to be regarded in this process as a thing in itself, just as it was before the Statute of Wills transformed the world of inheritance when it first appeared in sixteenth century England. In fact, your estate is not a 'thing in itself.' Instead, it is an intertwining set of relationships between you, your ancestors, your children, and generations of your children yet unborn.

Those relationships cannot be quantified mathematically. They cannot be folded into a balance sheet. They defy scientific inquiry. And yet, it is precisely those relationships—and the conditions that will either undermine them or nurture them and make them strong enough to survive for generations—that will determine the success or failure of not just your estate plan, but, more importantly, of your family itself.

CHAPTER THREE

I, Being of Sound Mind...

"Your last will and testament is
the wrong place to do your parenting"
The Authors

When the founder of one of America's largest frozen foods companies died in the mid 1990s, a fortune estimated at over $500 million dollars was to be distributed among a small group of heirs: his second wife, their three children, his brother and a cousin.

He had been meticulous, almost fastidious, in the management of his business affairs. Workers on the plant floor would tell you that he could walk past a flash-freezing conveyer laden with tons of washed peas, and tell you, within a twelve-ounce box or two, exactly how many packages of frozen peas were in that unit.

His daily life was a model of precision and efficiency. Up at 5:00 a.m. for a one-hour swim, followed by breakfast at the club, then a staff meeting at 8:00 a.m. sharp. Every minute of his day at the office was focused and productive. He required comprehensive production reports daily, and he could account for every pea, kernel of corn and bit of broccoli from the time it left the farm until it was washed, prepped, frozen, packaged and palletized to the loading dock.

He managed his personal life in much the same fashion. In fact, the only blip in his seventy-seven-year personal life was his divorce from a first wife when he was thirty-five. Other than that, he and his second wife had raised three children, served in their church, and supported local charities with a quiet dignity that was the envy of all who knew them.

His estate and business succession planning had been no less carefully considered. A team of seasoned CPAs, investment managers and attorneys crafted a state-of-the art plan that took several years to complete. To see all of the contracts, agreements, trust documents and other legal and financial instruments that comprised his plan laid out on one table was an impressive sight. The frozen foods king kept a set of the plans on the credenza in his office. They sat there for several years, three thick binders larger than the New York City phone directory. It gave him peace of mind to glance over at them from time to time. It was a matter of some pride to him that immediately following his death his estate would be settled seamlessly, and with great decorum. Dignity and efficiency. The hallmarks of his business life would be the legacy of his personal life.

(And now, the sound of a whoopee
cushion being deployed with great gusto!)

In fact, within hours of his death, attorneys representing just about everybody the frozen foods magnate had ever brushed up against in life were in line to file briefs at the county courthouse. Stays. Writs. Pleadings. Injunctions.

His three-volume estate plan, with its elaborate mechanisms focused on minimizing taxes, was pronounced dead at about the same time he was. His first wife, whom he had not seen or talked with in over forty years, wanted *something*. The oldest son wanted *everything*. The middle son wanted *more*, the daughter's husband (no doubt deep in grief over the loss of his father-in-law) decided they should hold off on their own divorce proceedings, and instead convinced her she should have a role in managing the company. His cousin's demand for money was based on a claim that he had secretly helped invent the company's first flash-freezing system, while the brother figured he had been out on the loading dock long enough to deserve a spot in the head office.

As for the grieving widow, her instructions to the phalanx of lawyers assembled to join in battle was short and simple: "To hell with them all. None of them deserves a dime."

At this writing (fall 2005), the family and their legal representatives are still slugging it out. Several million dollars have been spent (so far) on legal and accounting fees. The traditional Christmas gathering at the parents' house has been on hold for the last eight years. And none of the kids is talking to mom—let alone to one another.

The advisors to the frozen-foods baron had constructed a great plan. What no one had done, what few ever do, was to spend an equal amount of time and energy *preparing the heirs* for the receipt of that plan.

Welcome to the real world of estate planning—American style.

Over the past century we have developed a sophisticated system of death planning built upon a single overriding premise:

The goal of estate planning is to preserve accumulated assets from taxes.

To be sure, we could add that its purpose is also to mitigate attorneys' fees and administrative costs, but the central objective of death planning in America has been, and remains, to preserve the assets accumulated in the present generation for the succeeding generation.

According to Paul Schervish of Boston College, at least forty-one trillion dollars will pass from one generation to the next by the year 2044.[1] It's probably fair to say most of it will be passed from this generation to the next with the same mindset: *protect the accumulated assets.* It's also fair to say that the success rate of those traditional plans (when measured out across two to three generations) will be about the same as the success rate of parents in getting their three-year-olds to eat the mushy *'freezer to microwave'* vegetable medley that our frozen food friend pioneered.

Which begs the question: if the track record for traditional estate planning is so bad, why has it been the dominant planning process?

Imagine a powerful steam locomotive barreling down the track, with a clear sky, a strong tailwind, and an energetic crew feeding the boiler nonstop. An engine that continues to gather momentum as it climbs to the highest mountain pass with only a slight reduction in speed, then gathers more speed and energy as it descends to the valley below. It is unstoppable. There is abundant fuel, and fresh crews stand ready to relieve the boiler stokers whenever they tire. The engineers and crew never look back. Their eyes are fixed only on the distant horizon. There is no end planned for the journey. They just keep going.

This is a quintessentially American attitude. It fueled the growth of the most dynamic economy the world has ever seen. Through boom and bust, war and peace, the energy behind the American locomotive has never faltered.

In *"The Greatest Century That Ever Was,"* Stephen Moore and Julian L. Simon wrote:

> *More financial wealth has been generated in the United States over the past fifty years than was created in all the rest of the world in all the centuries before 1950. Fifty years ago, real financial wealth was about five trillion in 1998 dollars. By 1970, that financial wealth had doubled to roughly ten trillion dollars. Since then the value of Americans' financial wealth has tripled to over thirty trillion. When we combine this burst in financial assets with the sevenfold real increase in housing equity owned by Americans, we discover that the nation's assets have risen from about six trillion to more than forty trillion dollars in real terms in the past half century.* [2]

America has been, and continues to be, an economic engine of prodigious proportions and astounding output. By any material standard imaginable, the quality of life today far surpasses that of one hundred years ago.

Wages? In 1910, the average hourly pay for a skilled worker (in today's dollars) was $3.43. Less than minimum wage today. By 1950, that hourly rate had increased to $9.70 per hour, and today, the average manufacturing wage is $12.85 an hour, even higher when you account for benefits like health care, retirement plans, vacations, etc.

Productivity? Agricultural production is five to ten times higher than what it was seventy-five years ago, and real per capita gross domestic product has risen from $4,800 to $32,000. We're working fewer hours, too. Your grandfather didn't exaggerate about that; in 1850, the average work-week was sixty-six hours. By 1910, it was fifty hours. Today, the American worker averages just thirty-five hours per week on the job.

Leisure? We have twice as much leisure time as our great-great-grandparents, and, of course, luxuries they couldn't begin to imagine-from flush toilets and indoor showers to air conditioners, microwave ovens, DVD players, and ever more powerful computers.

That's not to say we don't have our share of problems as we enter the twenty-first century. For every benefit there has been an equally significant cost. But, from a purely material standpoint, this much is certain: we have made extraordinary progress in the past century, and that progress has brought incalculable benefit to all of us—regardless of income level. There is simply no comparison between poverty as it exists in America today, and poverty as it was (and still remains in many parts of the world) a hundred years ago.

Growth in Material Wealth: A Very Long View

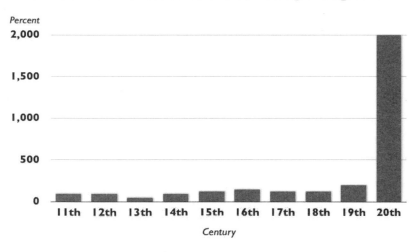

Source: Professor J. Bradford De Long, University of California, *Slouching Towards Utopia*

The above graph shows that the growth in material wealth has been explosive. In the spirit of *"a picture is worth a thousand words,"* it also demonstrates why this book is so important now.

So, in answer to the question, the estate planning system in America is the way it is because the system is the natural offspring of a century of amazing economic progress and boundless opportunity. Through the rigorous application of sweat and intellect, thousands of people rose from poverty to amass enormous personal fortunes in the late 1800s and early 1900s. People like Commodore Vanderbilt and John D. Rockefeller, Andrew Carnegie and J.P. Morgan. Leland Stanford, Colis P. Huntington, and Jay Gould.

The world had never seen wealth of this magnitude earned so quickly by so many. It took fewer than thirty years after the end of the Civil War for a uniquely American version of 'nobility' to emerge. Men who could make presidents. Their pronouncements on political or economic issues could send shivers of fear rippling through the national economy.

When J.P. Morgan decided to establish an umbrella corporation for American steel, he knew he first had to buy out Andrew Carnegie, who owned the most powerful steel company in the world. In 1901, Morgan asked Charles Schwab, the President of Carnegie Steel, to find out whether Carnegie would be willing to sell. Schwab went to see Carnegie on the golf course and presented Morgan's idea. Carnegie replied that he would think about it overnight, and, the next day, he returned with a piece of paper on which he had written in pencil, $480,000,000. That would be the selling price.

Schwab took the piece of paper down to Morgan on Wall Street. Morgan took one look, nodded his head, and said, "I accept this price." It took Morgan only a few weeks to put together a syndicate that purchased other steel companies and railroads and ore lands and steamships and barges. He capitalized U.S. Steel on March 3, 1901, at $1.4 billion. It was the largest corporation in the world.

(When you realize that the entire federal government was spending only about $300 million a year in 1901, and Carnegie's asking price was considerably more than that, you get some appreciation of the size of the fortunes these tycoons held and the kind of power that much wealth represented.)

By 1925, there were more mansions per capita in Rhode Island, New York and Massachusetts than in any of the great cities of Europe. The families of the great bankers and industrialists lived a gilded life of parties, theatres, and world travel. The New York Times referred to the founders of these fortunes as *"colossuses astride the globe."* Their sons were *"kings-in-waiting."*

All that money. All that power.

And, ultimately, all that misfortune.

Unfortunately, there was no relationship between the ability of the founder to make the fortune, and that of the children to develop a healthy relationship with the money. Andrew Carnegie's religious faith led him to the conclusion that such wealth should be put to use for the betterment of humanity; he subsequently gave most of his money to public libraries and other charities. He had no illusions about the effect of unearned money on children. In a letter to a friend, Carnegie said:

> *"The parent who leaves his son enormous wealth generally deadens the talents and energies of the son and tempts him to lead a less useful and less worthy life than he otherwise would."* [3]

That condition could certainly describe many of the children of the American tycoons. William K. Vanderbilt (1849-1920), grandson of the Commodore, spent his time engaging in leisure sports such as yachting, auto racing, and horse racing. His summer home at Newport, Rhode Island, was modeled after the Petit Trianon at Versailles. It featured five hundred thousand cubic feet of white marble, and custom-made furnishings by J. Allard and Sons of Paris. He employed a summer staff of thirty-six maroon-liveried butlers, maids, coachmen, and footmen.

Vanderbilt's lavish lifestyle was extraordinary, at least for its excess. How he felt about the impact his family's wealth had on his own life was another matter. He wrote to a favorite cousin:

> *"My life was never destined to be happy. Inherited wealth is a big handicap to happiness. It is as certain death to ambition as cocaine is to morality."* [4]

The phenomenal burst of economic activity in the late 1800s produced huge personal fortunes, and the sheer dimensions of this newly-minted wealth created a demand for specialized managers to shepherd and protect it. The rise of the great tycoons and the evolution of a thriving middle class of professionals with disposable income in the late nineteenth and early twentieth centuries gave birth to a new class of professional money managers, personal bankers, investment strategists and attorneys. Their job: to grow their clients' personal assets and to protect them from the icy grasp of stockholders, competitors, and the government. With scant exception, it is exactly what financial and legal advisors to the affluent do today.

The accountants and attorneys of the early 1900s were not charged with, or concerned about, the behavior of their clients' children. Their labors were undertaken with pen and ink, computation pads and legal briefs. (Family counseling did not exist. And families kept their secrets in their closets.)

Their legal and fiduciary responsibilities were considerable–and so was the compensation. Some of the great investment and banking houses in America today were founded by the very accountants who once served the tycoons, who soon accumulated vast family fortunes of their own.

With the passing years, the tools professional money managers could employ on behalf of their clients grew in complexity. They also increased the emotional / personal distance between advisor and client. You can't do business on a handshake anymore. By the early 1930s, the accounting and investment management fields had developed elaborate, highly technical sets of operational procedures and rules to govern their professions and to set standards for their work product. In conjunction with the regulations of the new Securities and Exchange Commission and other regulatory boards and agencies, a bold new world of money management and financial and estate planning emerged. A highly regulated, formalized, quantifiable world.

In large part because of various security scandals, the effects of the Depression, and the increasing government regulation and oversight which resulted, the job of advisor to the affluent became an increasingly defensive profession. The take-charge, innovative, take-the-offensive kind of money management that characterized the period from the Civil War up until the 1920s was gone forever–even if modern advertising would have you believe the opposite. Financial and estate planners were now operating from a different perspective. Their jobs were to protect and defend. Defend the asset base against all comers. Protect profits from the government. Defend against potential lawsuits, unnecessary regulation, even against unwelcome and undeserving would-be inheritors. Defend against everything except the collapse and destruction of the family they served.

Traditional estate planning hasn't changed much since the Roaring Twenties. Tax policies come and go, and new financial products pop up in response to changing legal and economic circumstances. Through it all, advisors to the affluent have pretty much maintained a respectable arms-length distance from the client's personal life and values base. Their task then, as now, was to manage and defend wealth; and, until very recently, the health of the client's family itself was not a part of the 'wealth' equation.

That is changing. In fact, the areas of responsibility within which the estate planning advisor works is undergoing a major overhaul right now, starting with the rejection of the old idea that the client can be defined by the list of assets he or she owns.

As crazy as it sounds, advisors have never worked from the assumption that a family, like any organization, is more than the sum total of its parts. Many advisors look at the client's family from a mathematical, static viewpoint. That is, if (a) the purpose of estate planning is to protect accumulated assets, then (b) the distribution of those assets through the payout line known as the inheritors should be planned for with the same sterile objectivity as the plans made for reducing or eliminating federal and state taxes.

So, the net objective of most traditional planning has been to generate plans that will get as many goodies as possible out of the deceased's estate, past the IRS, and into the anxious embrace of waiting family members. Under this simple system, success is measured at the time the checks are made out to the inheritors. What happens the next day? Well… that just hasn't been the advisor's concern.

Anyway, the men and women who built the engine that is the American economy weren't in the habit of looking back—let alone to the side. What worked for their businesses would work for their families. As long as the locomotive boiler was stoked with fuel (money), their families would prosper and continue to move ahead.

But, we know that nine out of ten inheritances ultimately fail. Why is that? And how is it that with all that money and power behind them those family locomotives run out of fuel and get pushed off the track?

To understand why inheritances fail, it is a good idea to begin with the money itself. Lots and lots of it…

CHAPTER FOUR

Sudden Wealth

*"How long does the average recipient of an inheritance
wait before they buy a new car? Just nineteen days."*

New Car Dealer Association

O n a clear autumn morning in 1949, Jack Wrum stirred from his sleep under a park bench in Sausalito, California, just north of San Francisco. He bummed change for a cup of coffee, then headed down to Dunphy Park to see what the tides in Richardson Bay had washed up onto the beach the night before.

As he filled his burlap bag with tin, glass and bits of anything he might be able to sell, Wrum spotted what appeared to be a green wine bottle poking out of a mound of brown seaweed. To his surprise, the bottle was corked–and the cork was sealed under a thick layer of some kind of wax. Things were looking up! He usually preferred his wine before his coffee, but, on a day as beautiful as this, he was prepared to bend the rules of etiquette. Plopping down beside the pile of seaweed, he began to saw away at the wax and cork with his pocketknife. In a moment the old bottle was open. To his great disappointment, there was no wine inside. Instead, he found a piece of paper, rolled tight with a rubber band.

Wrum unrolled the note and read:

"To avoid confusion, I leave my entire estate to the lucky

person who finds this bottle, and to my attorney, Barry Cohen,
share and share alike.

Daisy Alexander, June 20, 1937."

Wrum may have been a homeless beachcomber, but he knew opportunity when he saw it. He pocketed the note and went in search of the first attorney he could find. Within weeks, the story unfurled. Daisy Alexander was Daisy *Singer* Alexander, heiress to the Singer Sewing Machine company fortune. When Daisy died, she left twelve million dollars, company stock, and a letter to her British solicitor instructing that her legal will would "turn up in good time."

And turn up it did. One evening several years before her death, Daisy walked from her London home to the center of a footbridge above the Thames River. She drew the sealed wine bottle from her coat and tossed it into the dark water. The bottle drifted down the Thames and was carried by currents up into the North Sea. The Barents Sea pushed it across the northern coasts of Scandinavia, along the rocky shores of Russia and Siberia, then down into the Bering Straits and into the Pacific Ocean, where it drifted south until finally, after nearly twelve years, it washed ashore in a clump of seaweed near San Francisco.

An expert in ocean currents testified that it would take about twelve years for a bottle to travel from London to San Francisco. The bottle was found eleven years and eight months after the date on the will. Daisy Singer's will was authenticated. Jack Wrum received six million dollars, plus ongoing income from his share of Singer stock. Not a bad day's beachcombing.[1]

History doesn't record what became of beachcomber Jack and his remarkable windfall, and that's probably just as well. The one recurring problem among people who have inherited money out of the blue is that most of them end up struggling to come to grips with the effects of 'sudden wealth.' That's because who we were the day before the inheritance was received, or the lottery winnings paid out, is who we are the day after. We have the same strengths, the same flaws, the same habits. Character is not *improved* by the sudden receipt of money. It is *revealed* by it. (That explains the new car in nineteen days. And, while you might have guessed as much, when we ask parents "What's the last thing you want your children to do when they get their inheritance, the overwhelming answer is: "We *don't* want them to go out and buy a new car!") If we didn't have a healthy relationship with money before we became rich, that relationship will only grow more problematic as we suddenly find ourselves awash in money, with ramifications that can ultimately destroy the things we love most.

To appreciate the potential danger and power that the sudden inheritance of money can have on a person, it's important to know that there are different kinds of inheritances that we can give or receive. Most of us think of things like property, stocks, bonds, or cash when we think of what constitutes an inheritance. Of course, lots of inheritance problems could be nipped in the bud if the inheritors simply understood that most estates consist of real estate and securities, not cash. Those securities are often closely held, part of the family business. So, the siblings they are about to go to war with over the estate assets just might end up being their partners in business.

For hundreds of years, estate planning has focused on these *financial* inheritances almost exclusively. But there is another kind of inheritance that we receive and give, an inheritance that is far more powerful, and ultimately more meaningful, than money. That is an *emotional* inheritance: one we receive over a lifetime from other family members, friends, teachers, religious leaders, coaches and other significant people in our lives.

There is a great difference between the financial inheritance we *may* receive from our parents or grandparents and the emotional inheritance we *will* receive no matter the size of their material estates. Metaphorically speaking, they are apples and oranges.

Financial inheritances are easy to understand: they are material and quantifiable. Traditional estate planning has any number of strategies to protect the assets from taxation in order to deliver the maximum amount to the heirs. In traditional estate planning, money is the exclusive focus, the guide-star, and the only real concern of the legal process. It is the beginning– and for most, the ending–of the estate planning cycle. Of course, since we know that most traditional estate plans begin to crumble almost as quickly as they shower assets on the heirs, one might be tempted to call money the time bomb inheritance.

Emotional inheritances are quite different. They are composed of the values that you experienced and absorbed from your parents, grandparents, and other important people in your life. These people of influence may have taught you these values explicitly, or perhaps you picked them up simply through living around them and interacting with them. It is this emotional inheritance (added to and enriched by your own life experience and living example) that you will pass on to your family and other people you know, *whether or not* you leave anything amounting to a financial inheritance. This emotional legacy is no less than the sum total of your life experience as evidenced by the values by which you lived. Values such as work, faith, philanthropy, and honesty.

You received an emotional inheritance from your parents or grandparents while they lived. Your own children or grandchildren are receiving theirs from you right now. The discovery, articulation and incorporation of these core values into the framework of your estate planning is what The Heritage Process is all about. The whole concept of wealth is redefined to include not only money and other financial assets, but also the values, virtues and ethics that make life meaningful, fulfilling *and* ultimately successful. In this values-based planning process, money is still important, but only in its function as a resource to help perpetuate the values that will keep the family strong and prosperous for generations.

There is a reason why nine out of ten inheritances fail. The best plan cannot compensate for an unprepared heir. When money is the primary focus of estate planning, inheritors often equate their self-worth with their net worth. Jessie O'Neill, author of *The Golden Ghetto: The Psychology of Affluence* (herself an heir in a wealthy family), describes the impact that a financial inheritance can have on people who receive a financial inheritance without an emotional inheritance—that is, money without meaning. She lists the following outcomes of the condition known as 'affluenza,' defined as a dysfunctional relationship with money, or the improper pursuit of it:

- Inability to delay gratification
- Inability to tolerate frustration

- Low future motivation

- Low self-esteem

- Low self-worth

- Lack of self-confidence

- Lack of personal identity

- Social and emotional isolation

- Feelings of depression, failure, anxiety

- Unrealistic expectations and lack of accountability

- False sense of entitlement

- Inability to form intimate relationships [2]

People who receive 'sudden' money without any accompanying values often become hoarders. Or, conversely, they may become habitual over-spenders, shopping with no concern for their dwindling bank balances. Quite often, they use money as a tool to control others, particularly family members. Controllers can devastate their children's lives, dangling money like a carrot on a stick to 'encourage' children to go to the right school, get the right job, or marry the right person. Many inheritors also use money to gain approval of others, including their own children. They may join exclusive country clubs, or buy a much-too-expensive home in an exclusive neighborhood.

We know of a man who had been the proverbial skinny, pimply-faced nerd at his high school, who went on to make a fortune developing shopping malls in California. So painful were his memories of being picked on and abused in high school that he decided to try to re-invent himself in the minds of all those who had tormented him for years. He rented a cruise ship for his twenty-fifth high school reunion, and chartered a 747 for more than three hundred members of his graduating class, with a spouse or guest, to fly to Italy, where they cruised the Adriatic Sea for ten days. As far as we know, none of those lucky classmates have continued any kind of friendship or relationship with him since the cruise.

The symptoms and manifestations of this dysfunctional relationship with wealth make up a pretty depressing litany of disorders. The whole idea of affluenza flies in the face of what most people believe their lives would be like if one day, just like Jack Wrum, they came upon the proverbial pot of gold. "If I only had money," the fantasy begins. "People would like me. I would be respected. I would be free to do whatever I wished, whenever I wished to do it. I could take charge of my life, and I would have a sense of absolute security. Nothing could intimidate me, and I would have power. Real power. Most importantly, I would be happy."

It's a great fantasy. An enormously seductive fantasy.

Imagine waking up tomorrow to discover that you have inherited one hundred million dollars from a long-lost uncle. You can immediately satisfy your every desire. You have the wherewithal to buy any home, any consumer toy, piece of art, luxury automobile, even companionship. Jet to Fiji tomorrow? Why not? Spring in the Hamptons? Dinner at Maxim's? Why not, why not, and why not again. Life is meant to be lived. Fully. That's the essence of the financial fantasy, after all. If the opportunity to indulge every fantasy, every whim, every physical or emotional desire should drop in your lap, what are you going to do? Brush it away like a hot coal that popped out of the fire?

(For starters, you might want to try to forget the Yiddish proverb that says *"If you want to know how God feels about money, look who He chooses to make rich."*)

Let's face it; the only thing the world celebrates more than money are the people who have it. In any survey of *'America's most admired people,'* high-profile media, sports and business celebrities always rank high. But, other than wealth, for what are these people really known?

Are they famous for their philanthropy? For their vocal support of education? Their vigorous stands against drug abuse? Their understanding and compassion for people from all walks of life? For being the kind of friends, husbands, wives, daughters upon whom you can really count?

They are famous because they are rich, period. Not one survey respondent in ten thousand could tell you in what these media darlings really believe, for what they stand, or what they have done for the betterment of the world they share with the 'little people.' It's certainly possible that their families could answer those questions. They may in fact be generous to a fault with charities and other worthy causes. As free-market supporters ourselves, the fact that they are wealthy is just fine with us.

It is the larger point we wish to make: the point that people's perception of the affluent is colored more by the idea that money equals virtue, than by the reality of what the affluent person did to get that money, or for what they actually use it. For many people, the possession of gobs of money is the greatest, noblest achievement one can aspire to. In such a culture, should we be surprised if heirs get their priorities out of kilter?

The trendy shops along Rodeo Drive in Beverly Hills sell the rarest and most expensive baubles imaginable. South Beach plastic surgeons can turn a toad into a prince (or at least a shiny-faced likeness of one). But boutiques don't sell character, and plastic surgery can't remove our hidden insecurities with the touch of a scalpel. We are, each of us, the product of a lifetime of experience that no amount of cash falling on our heads from heaven can alter. The sudden receipt of *'money without meaning'* only magnifies the personal weaknesses with which each of us live, no matter our station in life.

There is no denying that money bestows great power upon those who possess it. But there is a limit to what money can actually provide. Money will buy a luxurious bed, but it cannot guarantee a good night's sleep. It can buy a magnificent library, but not brains, nor the discipline to educate yourself; gourmet food but not a healthy appetite. Money can buy designer clothing and jewelry, but not true beauty. It can purchase a house, but never a home; state-of-the-art medicine but not health; luxuries but not culture or taste; temporary amusements but not lasting happiness; religion but not salvation. Money, in fact, can buy a ticket to just about everywhere but heaven.

People who receive sudden wealth like to tell themselves and their friends that their new found treasure hasn't changed their perception of themselves. And that may be true. But money certainly changes the way others will perceive you. An ancient Chinese proverb says: *If you are poor, though you dwell in the busy marketplace, no one will inquire about you; if you are rich, though you dwell in the heart of the mountains, you will have distant relatives.*

What does affluenza look like in real life? Meet a real client, named William. He comes from a middle-class family in Portland, Oregon. His father was a pipe fitter; his mom took in sewing and laundry. William excelled in high school, but his family couldn't afford college, and his scholarship only paid part of his tuition. So William worked his way through school. During the school term, he worked as a waiter, a short-order cook, and a plumber's assistant. Each summer he worked as a deckhand on an Alaskan fishing boat. He even picked fruit and vegetables in Oregon's fertile Willamette Valley farms to pay his way.

His work ethic, his enthusiasm and his drive were just amazing. No one was surprised when William graduated at the top of his class. He went to work for a machine parts manufacturer and took on every job they had; from maintenance to machine operations, outside sales to personnel management. Eight years later, he started his own manufacturing business in a small rented warehouse. Today at age fifty-nine, he has a net worth in excess of $10 million dollars.

Like many people who become successful through hard work and great personal sacrifice, William made a vow: his kids would never have to work as hard as he did. They wouldn't have to give up parties and football games, and they wouldn't have to buy clothes at Goodwill. They would have everything he didn't—and more. They spent summers at expensive camps and had credit cards by age fourteen. At sixteen they were given keys to their own cars. When it came time for college William made sure they would be able to concentrate on studies and social activities; none ever had so much as a part-time summer job.

In short, William made sure they grew up without a single one of the experiences that had shaped his own life. So, how have the children done?

It has been a bumpy road. William's three children, ranging in age from twenty-three to thirty, have two failed marriages, one bankrupt start-up business, and several drug and alcohol rehab visits between them. Two did graduate from college, but only one currently works at a full-time job. William has tried to bring them into his business, but they just aren't interested. He is so distressed by his children's lack of ambition and motivation that he has decided to sell his business rather than leave any part of it to them.

William's situation is more the rule than the exception among first generation wealth builders. When his story (with names changed to protect everybody) is told at estate planning seminars, planners, attorneys, non-profit officers and others nod their heads in understanding all over the auditorium. They have all seen 'Williams' in their practices. Nevertheless, like most traditional financial and legal professionals, their focus is on minimizing risk and growing wealth, not on helping client families identify values that can be used as a foundation for estate planning.

We've all heard about—or seen firsthand—the effects of sudden wealth on people, even if only on a small scale. We read about the tire store worker who wins millions in the lottery and is broke two years later. Or the teenager who gets a small inheritance from a grandparent and blows it on clothing and parties in a matter of days. As for movie stars and rock divas, well, the less said about their excesses, the better.

Still, this is all anecdotal evidence. Is there really that strong a case for a cause and effect relationship between the receipt of sudden wealth and the onset of affluenza? Can't people like William's children—despite having no special training in money management or much life or work experience in the "real world"—learn to successfully manage wealth and keep their families intact on their own and avoid the Midas Curse?

Rod often tells the butterfly story to advisors who work with the 'Williams' of the world. It illustrates a basic truth about the root causes of affluenza.

A man sat on his deck, watching a Monarch butterfly struggle to break free of its cocoon. The butterfly twisted and turned, pushing its tiny body against the resilient walls of the cocoon. Its small mouth gnawed a tiny opening at one end, which it slowly and persistently worked to enlarge. Time and again, the butterfly pushed and poked and gnawed, only to fall quiet, exhausted from its efforts. Then, another push, another twist, then collapse. Over and over, the butterfly fought to be free of its cocoon.

After an hour of relentless struggle, the butterfly seemed to give up. It lay still for several minutes, with the tip of its head barely emerging from the elastic cocoon. The man decided that unless he intervened, the butterfly would die. He went inside his house and got a pair of scissors. He made a few delicate cuts along the length of the cocoon, and peeled it back from the body of the butterfly.

The butterfly quickly stirred and immediately unfurled its wings. But the man saw that the body of the butterfly was swollen and lumpy, the wings were shriveled and small. Even the characteristic brilliant orange and black hues of the Monarch were faded. The mis-shapen butterfly crawled around the deck for a few minutes, and then died.

The man wanted to understand why the butterfly had died, so he called a professor of entomology at the local university. The professor told him that in his attempt to ease the butterfly's struggle he had actually caused its death. For a butterfly to build the strength and stamina to live, the professor said, it had to fight hard to emerge from the cocoon. And the process of slowly squeezing out of the tight cocoon walls actually forces fluid from the butterfly's body and into its wings, enabling it to fly.

The man's intentions were understandable, said the professor. It is difficult to watch any creature struggle. And yet, it is only from the struggle that the butterfly achieves the essential characteristics and abilities it needs to live.

It is the same with people. What was the cliché we always heard as kids when we were forced to complete an unpleasant task? "It builds character." Clichés become clichés because they are generally true. Our character *is* shaped by the way we face the struggles in our lives. Especially in the way we deal with failure. The authors of this book have sat with hundreds of self-made affluent people, some with net worths in the billions of dollars. When they ask about the paths these people carved out on their road to financial success, there is one theme they hear over and over. To become successful, they are told, you need to learn to *fail well.* Learn to fail in a way that prepares you for greater success. Understand that learning and personal growth, skill development, courage, persistence, the potential for empathy and other important life assets, all come from your struggles, and especially from your failures.

If we seek to avoid challenges, if we shy away from setbacks, if we hide from the world or give up on our dreams when we fail, we will never learn the skills and abilities necessary to thrive and prosper, in both our business and personal lives. Experiencing failure gives us the opportunity to wrestle with the kind of challenges that squeeze life-giving fluid into our own wings and prepare us for successful flight in life.

It is important to note that William's problem is not that he does not love his kids. Clearly, he wants the best for them. He just never realized that the very values and ethics that brought him success—like hard work, sacrifice, and goal-setting—are the most valuable assets he possesses. How—or whether—he transmits them to his children is the single most important determinant of how successful they, and later their children, will be in building strong families of their own and in managing and growing the material assets they will be given.

For estate planning to succeed across generations, and for families to remain strong, the emotional inheritance must be identified and communicated to the inheritors. (John L. Levy, a psychological consultant who specializes in the problems of inheritors, says that most of the problems in inheritance could be prevented if people simply *talked* with their parents about these issues before they die!) That emotional inheritance becomes the framework for planning that puts *family* before *fortune* by focusing on the things of value, rather than on the value of things. As a result, the money remains a tool—not a cure, not a fix, not the answer to a prayer—and not the focus of the estate plan. And the purpose of that tool is simple: to support a family vision that reflects, honors and supports the values that helped earn the wealth in the first place.

Remember that forty-one trillion dollars that will pass from one generation to the next by the year 2044? That transfer—the largest asset shift in the history of the planet—can enhance the lives of families, strengthen their relationships, support the causes in which they believe and benefit countless philanthropic organizations.

Or, it could really make the day of those boutique owners along Rodeo Drive.

PART II

CHAPTER FIVE

Where Are You Now?

If we would have new knowledge,
we must get a whole world of new questions.

Susanne K. Langer

Jedediah Smith was a young man in a hurry. And on this day, September 15, 1826, he was also in big trouble. The twenty-seven year old mountain man and explorer leaned over the edge of the rock-rim canyon and peered off into the distance. Behind him the sun was just beginning to peek over the jagged mountains. Directly ahead, the barren landscape of the Mojave Desert stretched for miles to the western horizon, purple and blue in the clear morning light.

Smith's men, seventeen of the hardiest fur trappers and scouts in the territories, were stirring. The camp was coming to life. In a few minutes, the conversation that had begun around the campfire the night before would be picked up. Only today, Jedediah's men were going to want answers.

Exactly where are we? Where are we going? How are you going to get us there?

Smith was no stranger to those kinds of questions. At the age of twenty-two, he signed on with an expedition to travel to the Upper Missouri and trap beaver. A year later, he led another group deep into the central Rockies where he rediscovered the forgotten South Pass, the key to the settlement of Oregon and California. And tomorrow he would begin the last leg of the journey for which he will always be remembered: the first American to travel overland from the east, through the Great Basin, and then by foot through the brutal Mojave Desert (where it was so hot that he and his men had to bury themselves in sand during the day to cool down), to California and the Pacific Ocean. By the time he was cut down by a Comanche war party near the Cimarron River in New Mexico at age thirty-three, Smith had traveled more extensively in unknown territory than any other single explorer in U.S. history.

Smith's life was made up of critical moments in which he had to ask himself (even when his men were not pressing the issue), "Where am I?'" Imagine *walking* from Salt Lake to Los Angeles without bottled water, air conditioning, convenience stores, motels, roads, not even a map. (The tarantulas, fire ants, rattlesnakes, scorpions and other desert creatures along the way might inspire you to ask not only "Where am I?" but, "What am I doing here?")

"Where am I?" is a seminal question, whether it's asked on freshman philosophy exams, or, far less frequently, by the handful of men who will actually relent and stop at a gas station to ask for directions. It is a question that frames important issues in life (career, marriage, family, finances, faith), one that inspires the most important thinking, and the most crucial conversations, we will experience in our lives.

It is also the first question people ask when they get down to the chore of developing their traditional estate plan. As you'll see, the values-based legacy perspective of The Heritage Process expands this question to "Where am I, and where is my family, and where will they be in the years ahead?"

Most people are familiar with the 'life planning' checklists that attorneys and financial planners provide for their clients. It's a good idea to have them and to keep them up to date (and easy to get to). They list the documents, policies, plans and instructions that make up the paper trail of estate planning. You probably have completed at least some of these:

Your Last Will & Testament

Durable Power of Attorney

Medical Power of Attorney

Trust Documents

Business Succession Plan

Life Insurance Policies

Deeds

Beneficiary Designations

Your list may be shorter, or much longer, depending on your family, financial and business circumstances.

For most families, the documents that make up the traditional estate planning package are the proverbial *'last nail in the coffin.'* They focus on endings, closure and finality. They mark the passage of a life, not the beginning of a legacy. Estate planning documents do the work of wrapping up old business (not the most pleasant way to phrase it, but accurate from the point of view of the professionals who are charged with distributing the dearly departed's assets) with an eye to dotting the i's and crossing the t's one last time.

Once the provisions of the will have been fulfilled, and the distribution of the assets has been accomplished, the thick manila file that represents the last vestige of the legal presence of the deceased person on earth can (and almost always will!) be sealed, boxed, filed and forgotten.

The unfortunate truth for most people is that when the file snaps shut for the last time on the folder bearing their name, it also snaps closed on their legacy.

The idea of legacy lies at the heart of this book. Understanding what a legacy is, and how you can achieve a lasting legacy that will benefit your family for generations, is where our conversation is headed. The journey to the creation of a significant legacy begins the way all important journeys do, with the same question that Jedediah Smith's men confronted him with on that chilly September morning: "Where are we right now?"

The series of assessment questions below have no right, wrong or perfect kinds of answers. They are designed to clarify your understanding of how the people in your life are actually prepared to implement your most important wishes when you are gone.

Where Are You Now
Personal Assessment

Please respond to questions using a number from 0 to 5. 0 means *not at all, absolutely not,* or, *I don't have a clue.* 1 means *I'm starting* or *a little bit* or *sort of,* all the way to 5, which means *absolutely, completely, totally.*

Response   *Question*

_____   How far along with your traditional estate planning (wills to trusts, etc.—see list above) are you?

_____   Are the documents kept up to date to reflect changes in your life and circumstances?

_____   Can your spouse (or other inheritors) easily access that information?

_____   Did you begin your estate planning process with any specific long-term plans for your family beyond, or in addition to, the distribution of financial assets?

_____   If the answer to the above question was a 4 or a 5, did you communicate those wishes clearly to each of your financial and legal advisors?

_____   Did you communicate them to your spouse?

_____   To your children?

_____ Your grandchildren?

_____ Did the advisors (lawyer, CPA, CFP, etc.) who prepared your planning work in concert, that is, as a real team, including holding meetings at which all of them were present and working from the same agenda?

_____ Have you had in-depth conversations with your *spouse* about the contents and design of your estate planning documents?

_____ Have you had in-depth conversations with your *children* about the contents and design of your estate planning documents?

_____ If you own a business with a partner, to what degree are you comfortable that, in your absence, your partner will employ the kinds of values and ethics in his / her decision-making that you would have used ?

_____ If you own a business with your partner, please ask your spouse this question: how comfortable are they that in your absence your partner will treat them with respect and honesty?

_____ Regarding your spouse's reply: is that what you thought he / she would say?

_____ Do your children know the story of how you accumulated your wealth?

_____ Do your grandchildren know the story?

_____ Have you shared that story with your inheritors in any kind of formal way (family meeting, video or audio tape, written story, etc.)?

If your children were asked to identify the values (like faith, strong work ethic, family time, honesty, etc.) which they believed you would say are most important to you in your life, would their list and yours be pretty much the same?

(For example, if you believe your daughter Alexa could do a good job of listing the values that you would say are the most important in your life, you would fill it in like this:)

4	Daughter	Alexa
_____	Son	_____
_____	Son	_____
_____	Son	_____
_____	Daughter	_____
_____	Daughter	_____

If asked to list the values that are most important to them in their *own* lives, how closely do you think your children's list would mirror yours?

_____	Son	_____
_____	Son	_____
_____	Son	_____
_____	Daughter	_____
_____	Daughter	_____
_____	Daughter	_____

_____ How important do you believe it is for your children to understand the relationship between the values you have lived by and the success you have enjoyed?

_____ Would you say having your children understand the relationship in the question above is just as important as their understanding the terms and conditions of the estate planning documents with which your assets will be distributed?

_____ How important do you feel the money you leave will be in helping your children, and their children, live healthier, fuller and more productive lives?

_____ How good a job have you done communicating the values that are important to you to your children?

_____ Do you know your maternal or paternal great-great grandfather's first name?

_____ Would you like your great-great grandchildren to know yours?

What does this mean?

As we said at the outset, this was not a test. It simply provides an opportunity to become better acquainted with your feelings and attitudes about the planning process. If you add your total response score up, and then divide it by the total number of questions that applied to your situation, though, you will get an average score per answer, on the scale of 0-5.

If your average answer was a 4 or a 5, you have done a remarkable job of communicating with your family about what matters most to you in life. They have a crystal-clear understanding of everything they need to do when you go to your great reward, and they have demonstrated a complete and thorough appreciation of the values by which you lived, and how those values helped you achieve your success. (Or, maybe your calculator just jammed.)

At the other end of the spectrum, if your average answer score was a 0 or a 1, it's time to get out the picks and shovels and begin the site preparation work for your personal planning foundation. Some kitchen table time with your family would also be a good idea.

The truth is, when most people begin to work on these kinds of questions with a qualified advisor, their answers are often not what they would wish them to be. They have not built a solid foundation of communication with family members. Helping them get to the place where their answers reflect what they really want for their families is what The Heritage Process is all about.

You might think that some of the questions were a little unusual, at least in the context you are used to when it comes to estate planning issues. You're right about that. The Heritage Process is not intended to supplant, or even compete with, traditional planning. That is not its function. The Heritage Process asks questions that traditional planning does not ask because traditional planning does not take a stand on the future of your family—its only focus is on the distribution of your assets. To put it bluntly, traditional planning ends when you do. Planning enhanced by The Heritage Process endures for generations.

Traditional planning is properly focused on transferring assets. The beans (your assets) are counted, divided and distributed. End of story. (Also the end, for the most part, of the involvement by the advisors who set up the plan.) The Heritage Process is about transition. The beans may still be counted, and distributed, but within the framework of a vision of a family plan in which the purpose of the assets is to strengthen multiple generations of your family in all of its interactions, both personal and business.

Like Jedediah Smith looking out across the vast Southwestern desert and envisioning his goal at the Pacific Ocean, The Heritage Process looks into the future of your family and envisions the enduring role of your values as a living reservoir in their lives. The Heritage Process does not come to a halt when you do. That's when it really begins.

Now, we'd be the first to agree that when you ask the question, "Where am I today in my planning?" it's a lot easier to get fast, snappy answers from the traditional planning side. Last will and testament? Well, it's either done or it's not. Family limited partnership-yes or no? Charitable Remainder trust? Check or no check.

Asking if your children can identify and articulate the values in your life that got you through the hard times, on the other hand, is a different ball game. But, which knowledge will better serve your children when one of them is facing a terrible crisis in his or her own life? Differentiating between codicils in a will? Or recalling that mom and dad faced some tough times themselves, and that they got through them with faith, determination, grit and hard work?

There is a great scene in Mark Twain's American classic, *Tom Sawyer*. Tom and his best friend Huckleberry Finn are thought to have drowned in the muddy waters of the Mississippi. Their grieving friends and a few relatives gather in a small church for the funeral–along with the very much alive Tom and Huck. The boys have played along with the drowning idea for a couple of days, and now, they get the extraordinary opportunity to attend their own funeral. Hiding in the church choir loft, Tom and Huck listen as their brief lives are eulogized. The boys can't help but break into loud sobs, and they are discovered and punished. But what an image!

What would it be like to have a chance to fast-forward to your own funeral, to listen in on all the conversations, and then to be able to return to your current life?

"Where are you now?" questions transform into "Where were you when?" stories at funerals. Where were you the day Jack announced that he was getting married, the time he accidentally (maybe) punched his boss in the nose, the time in college he stayed awake for four days in an attempt to get in the record books? Remember how he kept his employees on the payroll after the fire even though they couldn't get back into production for three months? Mortgaged his house, sold the plane, cashed in retirement plans...

Would many of the conversations at the service, reception or wake after your funeral revolve around the 'stuff' you accumulated in life? (Well, except for the golf clubs and the airplane, perhaps.) That would depend on the guest list, we suppose; but, where family and friends gather to recall the life of a loved one, the talk goes deeper than stuff. It gets to the heart of a life lived fully through the telling of tales that illuminate not what you owned but what you valued.

When we ask "Where are you now?" we're really looking ahead to where you will be generations from now, in the hearts, the minds and the daily lives of those who come after you. Your great-great-grandchildren will not be raising their glasses in memory of your assets at holiday gatherings.

Their glasses will raise in unison to you, and your memory, and to the values by which you lived.

CHAPTER SIX

What Are Your Own, Unique Values?

In our family, as far as we are concerned, we were born,
and what happened before that is myth.

V.S Pritchett

For most of us, the quote above rings true. We know a lot about our parents. A little about our grandparents, and next to nothing about our great-grandparents. Even if you have done some genealogical research on your family tree, for the most part, it is just that: names and dates on the branches of a tree.

As you reflect on the current status of the plans you have for your family and your estate, many questions and concerns will pop up. That is the nature of the discovery process. In this context, the age-old question, "*Where* are we going?" is secondary to "*Whose* maps are we using?"

At the core of the Heritage Process is a remarkable journey of discovery. A journey into the past. Not in search of scandal or shame, though truth be told, plenty of both abound in all families. Instead, this journey seeks to identify your true family treasure. That is your values, from the mundane to the extraordinary, the ideas that guided your family from the Old Country to the shores of America. The same values that inspired and lifted up your grandparents and parents, the ones they instilled in you as you grew and that you now seek to impart to your own children. Also, the values you learned from other important people in your life: teachers and coaches, scout leaders and religious leaders, friends and their parents, and employers and co-workers.

In this chapter we're going to take a look at the values that have defined, guided and provided support and structure to you and generations of your family. You'll notice we haven't used the term 'family values.' If the loud voices of national politics should be hanged by the neck for any one transgression, (you may be thinking, "only one?") we'd probably vote that the noose should be wrapped extra tight because of the way they have hijacked the idea of family values to suit their own purposes. Values in and of themselves are politically neutral. Once they've been shrink-wrapped by political operatives and covered with hyperbole by pollsters, they take on a different cast. For our purposes, the term 'values' will refer to the kinds of principles discussed below—no politics allowed!

Let's begin with an understanding of values, and why it is so important that we understand how your family's unique values have helped to bring you and your family to where you are today.

In the simplest terms, values are the accepted principles or standards of an individual or group. They tend to be the kinds of qualities of behavior, thought and character that we regard as being intrinsically good. Plus, they should produce desirable results and be worthy of modeling by others. For families in particular, they are the things we regard as having ultimate importance, significance, or worth.

Values are often easy to recognize, but can sometimes be easier to demonstrate than to communicate. Hard work is easy to see with the eye. Faithfulness is not. It requires thought, reflection and understanding to appreciate. For most people, the values that define their lives are anchored in concrete belief; they are constants that do not change with the turning of social tides.

Values like honesty, sincerity, diligence and self-reliance mean the same thing today as they did when Dwight Eisenhower occupied the White House. At least they do to average folks. Not surprisingly, the government's definition of values has undergone considerable change in the past fifty years. A 1953 publication from the U.S. Department of Commerce defined values as:

*"The fundamental principles and beliefs that guide individuals
and groups, and provide resolute guidance about the manner in which
people should behave."[1]*

No fog there. Just clear, principle-based expression.

Now, fast-forward to 2003, and see how a more sensitive, inclusive government defines the same term. According to the USDA:

*"Values are <u>relatively</u> firmly held and socially shared positions
or expressions about what is good or right; they are abstract and
normative and are considered to be <u>somewhat</u> stable."* [2]

There wasn't much room for nuanced interpretation in the 1953 definition. 'Fundamental principles' and 'resolute guidance' speak for themselves. But the average teenager, armed only with a learner's permit, could drive a tank through the logic of the newer definition.

Each of us typically values many different things, some more highly than others. How important any one value may be to us will vary to some degree according to the prevailing circumstances in our life at that moment. For example, when you are in your younger, acquisition-oriented phase of life, you might place high values on things you cannot yet obtain. From material things like homes or cars to less tangible but equally important and desirable *conditions* like security, social status, etc. People tend to place great significance and invest real value into things they cannot readily have. As your financial circumstances improve and you can pretty much buy any material possessions or other trappings of social achievement, the things that you once considered of great value (and, of course, the greatest motivators imaginable!) lose some significance.

The relative importance of many of the things we once valued can more wisely be weighed as we mature. Some call this the *"grey hair index,"* where every strand of silver tells a story of a lesson learned. The things we cherish in the second half of our lives are less likely to change in value with the changing circumstances in the world. That does not mean so much that we are 'set' in our ways or unwilling to bend. Instead, it means that through hard experience we have come to recognize the things that *really* matter. And from this more focused vantage point one of the most important roles for values in our life emerges: they can provide a framework in light of which personal and family goals may properly be set, prioritized, and incorporated into your life planning. This is the essence of The Guided Discovery Process.

Of course, it all begins with the recognition of the values that are most important in your life that you want to make sure your family (and any other people or organizations you may impact) appreciate, understand, and continue to propagate. That's a story that begins before you were born. Long before.

The values that sustained a pioneer family in 1867 on the long trek from St. Louis to Portland, Oregon, were probably a lot more vividly experienced on a daily basis than they are in their great-grandchildren's lives today. Encounters with grizzly bears, ferocious weather, threats from Plains Indians—these were everyday events for families in wagon trains. They had to call on reserves of physical strength and emotional resolve that are hard for us to imagine. But, the values by which they lived in the Old West are by and large those by which you live. They can be a sustaining force, and a guiding hand, especially in times of trial.

To become a living part of the legacy you will create for your family, the values your ancestors passed to you, and those gained from important people in your life, must be identified, articulated and acknowledged by your family members.

That may not be as easy a task as it sounds. In his book, *My Life as a Man*, Phillip Roth says that it was a family joke that when he was a tiny child, he once turned from the window out of which he was watching a snowstorm, and hopefully asked, 'Momma, do we believe in winter?'

The legacy of your parents and grandparents, the gifts from your ancestors who emigrated to America, the feats they accomplished in generations past and present, and even the skeletons in the family closet, all have stories to contribute and meaning upon which to reflect. Like the child watching the blizzard out the window, we have to accept the historical reality of those who came before us, warts and all, if we are to understand the impact on our lives of the values by which they lived.

As you think about your own values, and from where they came, first imagine yourself seated in a great, vaulted hall. You are at one end of a very, very long oak table. At the left end, extending so far from you that you can only make out the dim outlines of faces, sit your great-great-great-great grandparents. Seated in long lines to your left are your other ancestors, including your own parents, who sit next to you. These are the men and women who fought the wars that shaped continents, who put the muscle and the brain into the Industrial Revolution, and who died at places like Little Round Top and Flanders Field and Iwo Jima. They tamed the Great Plains and built cities and schools and factories. They raised families under impossible conditions, and through the best and the worst that history wrought, *persevered* through the power of faith and the daily application of values that defined every aspect of their lives.

Your family. Gathered there with you, alive, brimming with stories of sacrifice and success, love and loss. Bound together by a thread of values that interlaces centuries, and that will survive your passing, and your children's, for generations to come.

You will do their lives a great honor as you reflect on the gifts they have passed across the years. And you will do your family a great service as you use those gifts to build your own family legacy.

When you can, grab the old family album, and flip to a picture of any of your grandparents (or great grandparents if you have photos going back that far). You have probably never given much thought to what kind of job they did transmitting the values they held dear to their children. In keeping with the custom of the day, they probably didn't *talk* too much about those values. (No Oprah, no Dr. Phil.) But they did *live them*.

You have the opportunity to do both.

CHAPTER SEVEN

How Will You Shape
Your Legacy?

One generation plants the trees; another gets the shade.

Anon.

Perry and Rod have guided affluent clients through the development of their estate planning documents for two decades. Wills and codicils. Living trusts, life insurance trusts and charitable trusts. Business succession agreements. Family limited partnerships and durable powers of attorney. They have prepared virtually every kind of traditional estate planning document, covering almost every conceivable contingency.

Their clients, who include some of the brightest, most successful and accomplished people in the country, often ask for special circumstance clauses to be included in their planning documents. They may have concerns about business transition structuring, asset liquidation to pay estate taxes, or the creation of trusts for children with special needs. In fact, over the years, clients have asked Perry and Rod to modify estate documents to deal with almost any financial or business situation or family circumstance you can imagine.

Except one.

"No one has come to my office," Rod begins, "and said, *'Rod, I really appreciate the way you've done my will and my other estate planning documents.   Man! That grantor retained annuity trust is something–and the way you crafted the reversionary interests clause, sheer beauty. Love the CRT structures, too.   I know we're almost done, and ready for signatures. But you know, there's one other clause I want inserted.   And this is really important to me to get down on paper–especially in a legally binding document.*

You see, building my manufacturing business took up an awful lot of my time over the years; I didn't get that much time with my kids and grandkids. But, I want to make sure they grow up to be good people. Honest and decent. I want them to respect their spouses and their own kids, and I think they should do something for their communities, too. Plus, I want them to know the value and satisfaction of a good, hard day's work.   What do you say? Could we squeeze those stipulations in somewhere between the asset distribution plan and the family limited partnership structure?' "

Rod smiles when he tells the story. He knows that on the face of it, a request like that might sound downright silly. Even so, he has had some clients come pretty close. One said, "Look, can't we structure my business succession plan somehow so that my son actually has to *show up* in person and do some *work*?"

Rod's answer: *estate planning isn't the place to do your parenting.*

It isn't the place to carve out your legacy, either. Estate planning has been– and always will be–a fixture of life in any society that permits the private ownership of property. There must always be formal mechanisms for the orderly transfer of property from one generation to the next. Private property is the proverbial glue that holds everything else together. What is worth considering, though, is the fact in the past several thousand years there have only been a few improvements made on the transfer process. From ancient Egypt to imperial China, from Victorian England to twenty-first century America, about the only thing that has changed is the terminology on the estate planning documents themselves. The intent of estate planning–to pass as many of the assets to the next generation as possible, and the mechanics by which it has been carried out–through a lawful, recognized process, have remained fairly static over millennia.

It is not as if every person who visited a lawyer in the past few centuries has been blind to the fact that their children would need more than money to lead fulfilling lives. What is fair to say is that for most of history, parents have assumed that what they left to their children in the way of material assets was the best, most important–and practical–legacy they could possibly leave.

For much of human history, that probably has been true. It has only been since the appearance of the modern welfare state in the past hundred years that most people were guaranteed, at minimum, an adequate amount of food, shelter and medical assistance to sustain life. Before the dawn of the twentieth century, there really wasn't much in the way of government assistance for the necessities of life. Personal responsibility was not a political catch-phrase–it was a fundamental requirement for survival. (We can cite any number of examples in history that show that for most people around the world, life was brutal, hard and short, until quite recently. It was only about one hundred fifty years ago, for example, that over a million people died in the Irish potato famine.)

So, the fact that the essence, the impetus, and the overriding purpose of estate planning has historically been to keep the money in the family not only made sense, it made perfect sense. A parent's first responsibility to his or her children is ingrained as deeply as any other moral imperative: for the protection, the provision and the maintenance of life.

There was no compelling reason to change the basic building blocks of the estate planning process as long as the purpose of that process was so pure and unconditional. It was enough that the legacy a parent aspired to leave was bread on the table and a moat around the manor house. You don't need a trial attorney, for example, to make the argument that a pioneer family on the Pennsylvania frontier in 1763 would benefit more from a keg of dry powder and a brace of good muskets than from a family roundtable discussion about philanthropy.

That is the historical context within which the American tradition and practice of estate planning emerged. The purpose of planning was to sustain the basic life necessities of the heirs after the death of the parents. Period. And the legal system delivered. State by state, a complex framework of estate planning law and practice evolved to codify the process by which estates would be transferred from one generation to the next. In doing so, the concept of legacy was tied indelibly to the ownership of private property.

The relationship between property and legacy has deep and highly visible roots. For thousands of years we have seen that when people of wealth and power wanted to be remembered, they usually set about to build something big, impressive and long-lasting the world would never forget. The legacies of Pharoahs were immortalized in pyramids and obelisks; that of the Renaissance Princes in marble palaces and commissioned art. These days, Hollywood producers vie for attention with their over-the-top monstrosity homes, and 'everyday' millionaires give a few million to get their name inscribed on the dining hall at their local state university. From Sumerian King to American robber-baron, the vehicle of choice for those wishing to leave a legacy has almost always had to do with property.

At the dawn of the twenty-first century, the cultural, economic and political landscape has changed to such an extent that the behemoth legal machine that powers the mechanisms of traditional estate planning is arguably out of step with the true needs of clients. Perhaps especially when it comes to the idea of leaving a legacy.

For those who haven't checked lately, it is probably not a bad idea to point out that homes no longer come with moats. Not many children have to chop kindling and stoke fires to heat bath water, not many armored knights pillage around local cities, and even the tabloid-crazed media would be hard pressed to find tens of thousands of people starving in American suburbs. The historical notion of *survival of the fittest* (despite its brief incarnation on bad prime time TV) seems archaic and a just a bit quaint in a world where food, shelter, medicine and education are cradle-to-grave entitlements.

The world has changed. In the past century the conditions of life for most people have improved dramatically and with blazing speed. Because of that, the ages-old social equation that said *"Legacy* equals *Property"* is simply no longer valid. It has not been true for some time. As proof, recall that ninety percent of all traditional estate plans, which hinge on the protection and transfer of property, will fail the inheritors. It is incomprehensible to think that the people who created the material legacies that eventually crashed down around their inheritor's heads wanted financial collapse and family chaos to be their lasting legacies.

In 2005, the Allianz Life Insurance Company surveyed baby boomers and their parents on a wide range of family and finance related issues. "Many people wrongly assume that the most important issue among families is money and wealth transfer–it's not," said Ken Dychtwald, the survey designer. "Non-financial items that parents leave behind–like ethics, morals, faith, and religion–are ten times more important to both boomers and their parents than the financial aspects of inheritance. In fact, seventy-seven percent of those surveyed (age forty plus) said the most important inheritance they could receive or pass on would be values and lessons about life." [1]

Despite that overwhelming sentiment, the survey also reported that fewer than one-third of those responding had actually done anything about translating those wishes into action. No conversations with parents or children, no family meetings, and no documents.

The old ways die hard; many people are still focused on digging a deeper moat around the castle, and filling the storehouse with grain as a means of providing a legacy for their children. The myth that the property you leave behind will be your ultimate legacy is a powerful one. It is easy to understand, particularly given the weight of history.

When we talk about your true legacy, your significant legacy, and how The Heritage Process helps you to formalize and communicate that legacy to your inheritors, we aren't suggesting that your property is 'off the table' in that process, or that you're going to disclose the entirety of your estate to your children or other inheritors. Your material wealth is still important, but primarily in its function as a tool to support the transmission of your real wealth—which are your values. Your personal legacy will be defined by the values you held in life, not by the value of your possessions.

Please think for a moment about any two people whom you admire greatly. One person who is living, and one who is not (this be can any person from history). When you think about them, what kind of thoughts come to mind? What are your memories of them, were they people you knew as children?

Perry describes a wonderful experience he sometimes has during the Guided Discovery Process with clients. If they spent much time with their grandmother as a youngster, Perry might say, "Describe your grandmother's kitchen." ("Kitchen," the person may think? "What does my grandmother's kitchen have to do with planning for my family?")

But when they begin to talk, wonderful memories surface. It might be the smell of home-baked bread, one loaf rising on the counter, the other ready to be pulled from the oven. Or early morning conversations seated at her simple Formica dining table. Perhaps even the day they realized that there was more to this woman than the quiet homebody their younger brothers and sisters knew. This was a woman who had lived a full life, with joys and heartaches that steeled her spirit, strengthened her faith, and infused her with an enormous reservoir of wisdom and grace.

Where, in the sea of memories you have of your own grandmother, do visions of her bank accounts come into play? Could you possibly attach a monetary value to the time you spent in her company? And if she were to appear to you right now, and tell you what it is she is most proud of about you, do you think it would have anything to do with your material wealth?

In Frank Capra's classic film, *It's A Wonderful Life*, Jimmy Stewart's character is given a tremendous gift. At the edge of despair, exhausted, discouraged and all but defeated at every turn in his life, Stewart decides to take his own life. He plunges from a bridge into an icy stream, only to be pulled to safety by Clarence, a bumbling angel (second class). Stewart is distraught that, like everything else in his life, even his attempt to kill himself has failed, and he wishes he had never been born.

His wish is granted, and for the rest of the movie we follow Stewart on a journey which most of us (at one time or another in our own lives) have secretly longed to take. What would the world be like had we never been born? How would the lives of those we loved (except the children we never had, of course!) have been different had we not been there to grow up with them, to work and play with them, to stand beside them in their difficulties, to share in their joys?   And what about our accomplishments? The businesses we built, the lives we changed, the people we employed, the causes we supported?

For the purpose of a great story, Jimmy Stewart got to see that had he never been born, the lives of just about everyone he knew, and nearly everyone else in his home town of Bedford Falls, would have suffered his absence enormously. Lives would have been destroyed or lost, businesses ruined, hearts broken, a town ravaged–all because one good man was not there to make a difference.

The theme of *It's A Wonderful Life* has been a staple of literature through the ages, and for good reason. Unless people feel their lives have some meaning, some worth and some lasting significance, there isn't much cause not to take the leap off the bridge into the dark water below. So kings have erected their monuments, and composers written their great symphonies. Each of us, to the extent that we are able within our spheres of ability, endeavor to do or make or leave something from our lives that is significant. Frank Capra's film showed that even a common man could touch the world in ways that created a legacy of lasting value. That is why the movie touches people so deeply.

Sadly, none of us will have the full-blown dramatic opportunity that Jimmy Stewart enjoyed in the film. But each of us has known someone in our own lives who lit a candle and carried it through the darkness with every step they took. A grandparent perhaps or a youth pastor. A scout leader, a coach, a teacher, boss or mentor. Someone who personified values, exemplified good character, touched us, instructed us, and guided us.

These are people, from your own life or from history, who passed a living legacy directly to you. What has that legacy meant in your own life? Have you shared the importance of the values they taught you with your own children, grandchildren or other people around you?

Imagine, for a moment, that you have just stepped outside to collect your mail from the post-mounted mailbox across the street. Your mind is focused on things happening at the office, so as you walk into the street you don't notice the fully loaded eighteen-wheeler barreling down on you at sixty-five miles per hour. Whack! And that's it. Curtains.

Tomorrow morning's _Daily Clarion_ newspaper prints a one-paragraph obituary article (next to a display ad for all-season radial truck tires, of course). Don't feel slighted by the brevity of the story. That's about as much room as the average 1950s B-movie star will get! Anyway, there it is, just four short sentences, in plain black 11 point Times New Roman type. Your life. Beginning, middle and slightly embarrassing end.

Unless you are a member of British royalty (or someone who insists on getting in the last word in any conversation), you probably haven't gone to the trouble of writing your own epitaph. It's not on the top of the chore list for most folks. We're going to change that right now. In fact, we'd like to give you an opportunity very few people ever get: the chance to write two versions of your life story.

Please take a clean sheet of paper, a pencil with a good eraser, and a deep breath. First, print your name, and under it your date of birth. Next to your date of birth, write the date of your fatal encounter with the chrome grill of the massive truck (how about tomorrow's date?). Then, compose no more than four or five obituary style sentences summing up your life. The who, what, where, when kinds of information you see in most obituaries. ("Phillip Jones was born in 1937 in St. Louis, Missouri, and graduated from high school in 1955. After a tour of duty in the US Navy, he attended UCLA, where he earned a BA in accounting. He started his own accounting firm in 1965, the same year he married Irene Martinez, with whom he had three children....." That kind of information.)

When you are done, share it with a few people. Your spouse, a child or a close friend. Ask them if the obituary sounds accurate. Then, ask them if that's what they would have written if they had been the newspaper reporter assigned to write about your life. If they are willing, ask them to actually write their version down. Don't give them hints or direction. Don't tell them you're reading a book about how values can be used as the foundation for your planning. Just ask them to write about you.

What they bring back to you probably won't look much like the formal obituary you wrote, or what the newspaper may actually write about you some day. Those who know you, and who love you, are much more likely to focus on the deeds of your life, not on the details. Their writing will be infused with memory and meaning. When they hand the obituary to you, don't be surprised if they're a bit self-conscious, even embarrassed.

When you read their version of your life story, you'll see it wasn't the company you built that they care to recount; it was that Christmas Eve you went without sleep so you could put everybody's bikes together. That's what they will always remember. It will not be your net worth that your children and grandchildren will tell their own children about when they share stories about you. It will be your human worth.

It is that human worth, built with values, lived through values, and evidenced as values in action, that will ultimately comprise your true obituary.

The Heritage Process helps people identify that foundation, to shape that vision, and to share it with generations of their family. To get a feel for what that process is like, here is that second opportunity to tell your life story to generations of your own family. This is a powerful experience, one that is worth keeping....

We would like you to write a letter to your great-great-grandchildren.

The purpose of this letter is to *'pass a torch'* to them. That torch is you. Think about what was meaningful in your life. What you did that was good, what you wish you could have changed. What you hoped they might discover to be true in their own lives, just as you did in yours. Please speak personally as you tell them things like:

> *"This is who I was, this is what I believed in, this is what I stood up for, this is what I did, this is the difference I hope I made, this is how I want to be remembered, this is what I really left my children, my grandchildren, and you."*

We appreciate this will not be an easy task. Remember that few people get this kind of opportunity. Give it all you have. Don't rush. Don't feel constrained by the direction we have given....This is your opportunity to communicate the things that mean the most to you.

One final thing: when you have finished this letter, place a copy alongside your other important papers, so that it will become part of the 'official' documentation of your life. Include the instruction that it be distributed to your heirs, including the admonition that the letter be read aloud and passed on to each succeeding generation.

That letter can become the key to the most important legacy you will leave. That is a legacy defined not by what it was that you achieved, but by what it was that you believed.

You do not have to leave millions. Or build monuments.

Sometimes, to leave a legacy, all it takes is a trip to the kitchen.

PART III

Initial
Presentation

Ongoing
Family Retreats

Guided Discovery

The
Heritage
Process™

Initial
Family Retreat

Your Vision
Statement

Implementing
Your Vision

CHAPTER EIGHT

Introducing The Heritage Process—
An Adventure in
Discovery and Meaning

W hat you have been reading about the failure of the inheritance side of the estate planning equation may or may not seem applicable in your life right now. More than one person has taken a look at The Heritage Process and asked, "Why should I care about what my grandchildren make of themselves? It's their life. Their choice. Let them live with the consequences of the decisions they make. I did."

It's hard to argue with the basic premise of that sentiment. We would be the first to acknowledge that personal responsibility is one of the pillars of a productive life. Whether or not this process is right for you and your family, it is certainly fair to question the underlying philosophy.

But, there is no getting around this fact: whether by design or by default, you *will* leave a legacy. Some trace of you will remain after you pass. It may be as faint and short-lived as the last snowflake of spring, or as strong and enduring as a mountain of granite. With what degree of impact you bestow that personal legacy on future generations is one of your life's most important decisions.

Unfortunately, due to procrastination, lack of time or motivation, or countless other distractions, it is a decision often left up to family members or friends, usually about the time they are picking out a headstone. Take a walk through an old graveyard and look at the weathered basalt columns and ornate decorative stones that mark many of the graves of sturdy, solid citizens whose only enduring legacy resides in that ton or two of solid rock. (The poet Robert Frost once wondered about the "inverse relationship between the size of the headstone and the size of the legacy.")

If, like many people, you have asked the question at the head of this chapter, "Why shouldn't my children and grandchildren make something of themselves, just like I did?" we would answer, *they should.* The question then becomes, how did you actually achieve your success? What tools did you have? Who encouraged you, provided you with opportunity, stood beside you, gave you valuable advice? Did you run into any trouble along the way? It could not have been an easy journey. The road to success has more potholes than pots of gold. Was your patience strained, your faith tested? At the end of the day, what was it that sustained you? The answer to these questions contains the perfect description of the true legacy you will leave.

So, we say that if being a self-made, self-motivated, self-reliant individual is an important value to you, one that has been of great benefit to you in your life, then it is also one of the values that can sustain and strengthen your children and grandchildren, just as it did for you. Have you told them? Do they understand what it took for you to get where you are today, in spirit, mind and heart, as well as in bank account? If they don't know the story, how can they ever appreciate the common sense, practical lessons you learned along the road to self-reliance? What will they reach for in their own lives and experiences when they face tough times if they don't have your example upon which to draw?

This line of questions, in a nutshell, explains the thinking behind The Heritage Process. We developed it in part to help people find an answer to those questions. There was nothing like it available for people who sought a structured, effective process to help them craft a significant, lasting legacy. We did not do it to engineer a platform to sell products (we don't), with creative 'leave-a-legacy' twists like many of the huge financial houses. Nor to practice psychotherapy. And especially not to provide tools so people could control their heirs from the grave.

Our objective was simple: to assist people who wish to pass their values, with their valuables, to the people they love and the causes and organizations in which they believe. Traditional estate planning did not, and could not, achieve those aims. It never will because that is not what it is designed to accomplish.

As we began the long journey of research and development, some of our colleagues argued that our plan would never work. Too fuzzy, some said. Too touchy-feely, another added. Many advisors had ideas, suggestions, reservations, and doubts.

But not one attorney, CPA, planner, or non-profit executive ever said such a process wasn't needed. Nobody took the position that, "The estate planning system ain't broke, so why fix it?"

On the contrary. The best, most successful and accomplished advisors in the nation, who between them represent many of the most affluent families in America, all agreed that the traditional system does a wonderful job of passing assets and minimizing taxes, and a terrible job of preparing heirs to receive their material inheritances.

Our task, therefore, was to develop and refine a process that could meet the 'show-me' test of the toughest advisors before it could ever be put to work for the clients they represented. It had to be based on solid scholarship, implemented by highly qualified and experienced advisors, and, most of all, it just had to make sense to the families who needed it.

There are more of those families every day. Within our lifetimes, the wealth of the United States has increased by a staggering amount - jumping from about six trillion fifty years ago to some thirty trillion today. According to Merrill Lynch & Co.'s *2004 World Wealth Report,* the number of millionaires in the United States (which the report defines as people with at least one million in financial or liquid assets) jumped by fourteen percent to over two and a quarter million people in 2003. In other words, one out of every one hundred twenty-five Americans is now a millionaire.

By way of comparison, back in 1900 there were fewer than five thousand millionaires in the United States—or only about one out of every fifteen thousand Americans at the time.

And it's not just the number of millionaires that has increased. Since the 1960s, median household wealth in America has nearly tripled, growing from $29,000 in 1965 to $86,100 in 2001 (the most recent year for which data is available)—meaning that while half the nation's households were worth

$29,000 or less back in the 1960s, today half are worth more than $86,000. [1]

The data, the research and our own experience clearly show that most inheritances fail. Gaining a consensus on that fact was never a challenge—there have never been any takers for the argument that traditional planning builds strong families across generations. But that fact alone wasn't enough to build a new kind of planning model; we had to *redefine* the traditional view of wealth to include more than money and assets. It had to consider the values, virtues and ethics that not only contributed to a client's material success, but also helped make his or her life meaningful and fulfilling. Next, we had to construct a practical, achievable framework that would promote family strength, unity, and community involvement, while encouraging individual excellence and achievement on the part of family members. Lastly, we had to make the process one which could be taught to, and repeated by, other professionals.

No small feat.

The greatest challenge of all? Learning how to foster an environment within which people would talk to their children about the most taboo, forbidden and mysterious subject in human experience. (No, not sex. That's actually the *second* most hush-hush topic.)

The great forbidden zone of family conversation is nearly always money. "There's a toxicity and secrecy around money in many families," says Charles Collier, senior philanthropic advisor at Harvard University and author of Wealth and Families (Harvard University, 2001). "As a result, parents fail to provide their kids with any type of financial education–how to invest, say, or how to use a credit card–or to prepare them for the decisions they may have to make about their fortunes. Plus, in many cases, parents are too busy making money and managing their assets to think much about the effect it all will have on the kids." [1]

As for the contention that ninety percent of all inheritance problems could be resolved if families talked about the money, that is true–sort of. Talking about the money in this context does not mean revealing the bottom line on the personal or business balance sheet. It's not about the size of the asset base—it's about what money represents.

Our goal in getting the family talking about money is for them to realize that money is a tool. Just a tool. A powerful tool, to be sure, but, one, like fire, that makes a better servant than master. Stripped of its aura of invincibility and curative powers (the 'money solves everything' syndrome), money may be seen for what it is: a resource to help strengthen your family through the values you recognize as your most important assets.

In the chapters that follow, you will see how our conclusions about the failure of traditional planning and inheritance and about money and values, have been forged into a dynamic process that is grounded on both solid academic research and real-world experience.

You will see:

- how the idea of focusing on things of value, rather than on the value of things, translates into multi-generational legacy plans designed to combat the 'ninety-percent world'

- how an active program of family philanthropy may be the most constructive means of building bridges between family members, and ensuring family unity, that has ever been envisioned

- the important role of traditional planning advisors, attorneys, charitable giving officers, CPAs as active participants in the creation and implementation of your plans.

THE HERITAGE PROCESS™

– STEP II –

GUIDED DISCOVERY

*A process of learning, whereby the student is guided
by another to learn from his/her own experiences.*

CHAPTER NINE

Your Guided Discovery

*Men go abroad to wonder at the heights of mountains, at the
huge waves of the sea, at the long courses of the rivers, at the vast
compass of the ocean, at the circular motions of the stars,
and they pass by themselves without wondering.*

St. Augustine

*People are usually more convinced by reasons
they discovered themselves than by those found by others.*

Blaise Pascal, 1657

The first step in The Heritage Process will take you on a journey unlike anything you have experienced. Through Guided Discovery, the Heritage advisor will provide a structure within which you can reflect on, share and communicate meaningfully about the values and traditions that have shaped your life. Throughout this Discovery, the legacy of family members who have passed on blend with the stories of parents and grandparents and other significant people in your lives, and with their hopes for their children. It is a place where old family stories come to light, and take on new meaning. Before we start that tale, though, let us finish up an earlier one.

We opened this book with the story of a terrible fire and of a man faced with a difficult decision. As flames surged up from the basement and engulfed the back of his house, Jack realized he had just enough time to run back in to grab a few things. Now, if there's one good thing to say about what it means to stare death in the face it is this: the greater and more proximate the threat to your life, the clearer your vision of what truly matters is likely to become. (There is a reason we use expressions like, *"there are no atheists in fox holes."*)

Jack first thought about grabbing important family financial records, or gathering up folders containing critical pieces of a big project for his office. He also considered rounding up the most valuable pieces of his wife's antique silver collection. But, as you'll recall, we didn't tell you what it was he finally took. We only told you that his wife was moved to tears by what he risked his life to rescue from their burning house.

Later, you were asked to put yourself in Jack's place. What would you take if the fire was roaring in your house right now, and you only had enough time to grab one quick arm load?

We can't be sure of your answer, of course, but in The Heritage Institute's office, there was a pretty clear consensus: everyone said they would take the family photographs that lined the hall. They acknowledged that tax and financial records are important and a real pain to have to replace. And losing a treasured antique collection would be difficult. But they all agreed that, in the washed-out and faded photos of the ancestors who preceded them, and the color shots of the children who will follow, is something infinitely more valuable than documents: family photos provide a connection to eternity.

You probably have one or more around the house. Up in the hall closet, under your bed, or stuffed into an attic trunk. Old binders, with cloth-covered cardboard covers, faint with the distinctive, musty aroma of age. You're careful when you lay them out on the kitchen table, and children are cautioned to turn the brittle pages slowly. Someday, you'll make copies. Someday, you'll scan them all into your computer, and add notes so that your grandchildren will know something about the faces that peer silently out at them across the decades. Someday.

To some people, the rag-tag assembly of subjects in the old photographs are little more than an embarrassing reminder of how unsophisticated their ancestors were. The grainy photos of simple, poorly dressed, weary-looking people only make them feel good about their own take-charge, speed-of-light modern lives with all of its technological conveniences. They know the names of many of the people in the photos, but others are complete mysteries. Who is that woman holding Uncle Carl's hand? Is that Great-Aunt Edna as a child? Why is grandmother standing next to that store? Where was that farm picture taken? I didn't know there was a farm in our family. As for what that fellow we think is our great-grandad was named, or what he did with his life..... unless there are hand-scribbled notes on the back of the picture, who knows? And let's not even get into what the old codger may have believed, or for what he fought, or what he sacrificed to provide for his family. How could we be expected to know that?

The truth is, if we don't see—and appreciate—that the old family album is a living history of the value and meaning of character, faith, endurance and hope every time we flip it open, we are missing one of our family's greatest legacies. The values by which your forbears and other important people in your life lived, are, without question, the most valuable and useful assets you posses. More important than real estate, investment portfolios, even cash. Because right there, in the unvarnished, honest faces of the generations who came before you, and the people who have influenced you, lie the keys to understanding everything you need to know to keep your family strong for generations.

Look again at the black and white photo of great-grandfather. The immigrant from the old country. He worked night and day to provide basic food and shelter to his family, sacrificing his own dreams so that one day his children would have a better life than he did. Photos of grandfather and grandmother, struggling to hang onto their farm during the Depression, sustained only by sweat and faith. Then mom and dad, with those silly grins, standing proudly in front of their first house. Even without pictures, you can create a 'photo album in your mind' filled with living images of the teachers, coaches, pastors, Boy or Girl Scout leaders, parents of childhood friends, and other significant people from your own past. This is your true asset base. These mental images and old photographs represent the source of your greatest strength. They are also the most enduring gift you will ever receive, or ever pass on.

The fact is, all of the investment advice from advisors and best selling business books, and all of the talking heads on TV money management shows, do not offer a fraction of the wisdom, the courage, the strength of character or the uncommonly good sense of the family, friends and other important people who have touched your life. The values in which they believed and by which they lived constitute the single most important resource you will ever have when planning for the future of your family.

The Heritage Institute was created out of a conviction that real success as a family doesn't come just by planning for the *future* but also from recognizing and applying the lessons from the past. In the end, your own legacy will be defined by what you have valued, not by the value of what you have owned.

The process of successful financial and estate planning begins with the recognition of those values, ethics and traditions that are unique to you and your family. They may have come from many sources, but, if your planning is to succeed (which by our definition, means keeping your family healthy and strong for generations), it must reflect and embody those values. They will sustain and guide your family in the future, no matter the size of your estate. Common sense tells us that. Research studies verify it. But it has only been in the past few years that qualified advisors arrived on the scene who could help families make the leap from that common sense conclusion to a practical, proven, nuts and bolts planning process built on a foundation of your unique values.

To help achieve a plan and a vision that can help your family thrive and prosper for generations, The Heritage Process begins with a remarkable tool called Guided Discovery, which is a process of learning in which you are guided by your Heritage Advisor to learn from your own experiences. Its purpose is to help identify and clarify the values that you and your family hold dear and then to use them to construct a framework upon which your ultimate financial plans will rest.

Simply put, Guided Discovery draws on the best of your family's past as a means to sustain and strengthen it in the future.

The initial discovery interviews are with you, and if appropriate, with your spouse or significant other. It is a powerful, and often deeply emotional experience. (However, it *is not* therapy!) That is why it is important that you work through the process with a qualified advisor. For many people, it is the first time that they have shared their reflections about their childhoods, education, work, significant people in their lives, children, their future, and other important issues in this kind of setting. (In a later step in the Process, The Family Retreat, the entire family will participate in a Guided Discovery.)

The Heritage Process begins with Guided Discovery, and Guided Discovery begins with the recognition that it is really through the ties that bind our forbears to us, and us to our children and grandchildren, that we achieve lives of purpose, meaning, and lasting significance. In Heritage planning, money is one of the tools that can help keep the real inheritance of values and meaning alive from one generation of your family to the next. But it is only a tool. (Kentucky Fried Chicken founder Harlan Sanders once quipped, *"You ever see a hearse towing a U-Haul trailer? What's the point of being the richest man in the graveyard–you can't do any business from there!"*)

The purpose of Guided Discovery is to identify things that, on the surface, might seem to be self-evident. But, as with most important truths, such is not the case. Consider the famous story of the reporter who asked the golf pro to analyze the pro's own swing. Something that had been second nature, as automatic as breathing, suddenly became nightmarish. The pro 'understood' the idea of the swing. In fact, didn't just know how to drive a ball, he was an acknowledged expert. But had never really thought about it; he just did it. He practiced and played–he didn't analyze. He worked with a rhythm of brain and body that seemed effortless–until, at the reporter's request, he began to methodically examine each mechanical component of his swing.

That's when his world collapsed. As he scrutinized each step in his swing, he realized that he really didn't understand the mechanics of how it all came together. In his attempts to analyze what had always been second nature, the adult learning center in the frontal lobes of his brain translated his inability *to figure it out* as an inability *to do it*. From that day forward, his swing was gone.

Guided Discovery helps avoid that kind of trap by providing truly new ways of looking at things you may have taken for granted or not thought about at all. Adults and children learn in different ways. A child would simply have brushed the golf question off and gone back to the game, no harm, no foul. Children are hard-wired to sop up information and experience like little sponges. Their brains distill and integrate those experiences over time without a sense of urgency or complexity. They see the world in black and white simplicity.

Not so with adults. The physical, chemical and emotional processes of learning are entirely different in adult learners. Physiologically, learning is the formation of cell assemblies and phase sequences. Children learn by building new assemblies and sequences. Adults mostly re-arrange the sequences they built as children into new structures. The good news is, that as child or adult, learning actually strengthens the brain by building new pathways and increasing connections that we can rely on when we want to learn more.

(And here's a fascinating note: recent research shows that at the neurological level, any established knowledge from experience and background appears to be made up of exceedingly intricate arrangements of cell materials, electrical charges, and chemical elements. Learning new information requires energy; but re-learning and un-learning requires even *more*. In other words, your brain expends more physical energy forgetting where you left your car keys than remembering where you put them in the first place!)

This first step in The Heritage Process uses Guided Discovery, in which you are an active, exploring participant. This is not like a lecture process in which you are just the recipient of a flow of information. People learn best when they make discoveries for themselves. Adults want to be the origin of their own learning and they will consciously (and subconsciously) resist learning activities they believe are an attack on their competence. They need some control over the what, who, how, why, when, and where as they learn new things. Most significant of all, adult learning has ego involved. And where ego leads, learning can be slow to follow.

Discovery is also the best way for you to learn because, although humans like the familiar and are often uncomfortable with change, we know that on its own, without any conscious thought on your part, the brain actually searches for and responds to novelty. It needs–almost craves–new "Ah-ha, I get it" experiences. (And yes, that may be why the dull memorization exercises in your high school geography class put you to sleep. Rote learning frustrates us because the brain resists meaningless stimuli. Research shows the brain actually shuts down different areas of activity when faced with waves of uninteresting information.) When we stimulate the brain's natural capacity to integrate information, however, we can assimilate boundless amounts. The key to that kind of learning? Easy. Discover it yourself.

Astronomer Carl Sagan said, "When you make the finding your-self–even if you're the last person on Earth to see the light–you'll never forget it." [1]

In Guided Discovery you have the opportunity to experience the highest order of learning–learning that wells up from within by virtue of your own interest and need. That's an all-too-rare occurrence for adults, say many experts.

What does the process of Guided Discovery actually entail? It is a two-phase process of questionnaires and personal interviews, designed to create personal and family wealth awareness. (Remember that the definition of wealth is not just about money!) The awareness developed through this process provides an understanding of your hopes, dreams, desires, goals, values and moral beliefs sufficient to create your *Vision Statement* (the focus of the next chapter.)

The questions begin with simple 'yes' or 'no' responses designed to help you focus on from where you came. As the interview progresses, the questions aim more at eliciting meaning and understanding, and will sometimes focus on people you may not have thought about for years.

Examples of these questions might include:

- *Who was the most influential person in your life during your teenage years?*

- *Why did you choose that person?*

- *What did you learn from that person?*

> • *Pick five or six words to describe that person. (i.e., caring, honest, hard-working, fun, ...)*

As you can see, the discovery process is designed to help you sift through a lifetime of experience. As you do that, you will probably find yourself coming to new levels of understanding and appreciation (those great, brain-stimulating 'aha' moments!) about yourself and your family. About how you became the person you are today. What role your parents, grandparents and other important people in your life played as you matured. How the best (and sometimes, sadly, the worst) of what those people contributed to your life has been filtered through you to your own children and grandchildren. What success and accomplishment and money mean to you. And, most importantly, what kind of clear, unambiguous legacy you desire to leave to generations of your family to come.

(Guided Discovery, it is important to note, is not about psychology or psychiatry, or working with significant dysfunction in families or individuals. Discovery is not analysis, and no attempt will be made to "fix" anything or anyone.)

After completing Guided Discovery with your advisor, you will have all the building blocks needed to begin translating your hopes, wishes, dreams, desires, and goals into a solid foundation of planning designed to sustain your family across generations. That foundation will be held together with a powerful cement fashioned out of the values by which you have lived, which you identified through the discovery process as essential to the health and prosperity of you and your family.

Next, this values-based framework will be shaped, structured, built upon and then communicated to your inheritors (and someday to theirs) through the creation of a document which will become every bit as important to your family as a Constitution is to the nation it defines.

Why a written document?

Well, what good is a vision if you don't publish it?

THE HERITAGE PROCESS™

– STEP III –

YOUR VISION STATEMENT

A meaningful and compelling vision of the family's dynamic and long-lasting pursuit of unity and of shared values, coupled with a clear focus on each family member's personal responsibility to leave a legacy of both self and wealth to the society in which he or she each lives.

CHAPTER TEN

Your Vision Statement

"There is one universal rule of planning: You will
never be greater than the vision that guides you."

Alliance for Non-profit Management

Why is it important to have a vision for the future? In an informal survey we conducted of the inscriptions that are carved into the marble and granite façades of public buildings, churches, monuments and memorials, one quote popped up more than any other. It is etched onto the door-posts of churches in Germany, libraries in the United States and Canada, memorials in Washington, D.C., and museums in New Zealand. Members of the British House of Commons pass beneath this quote as they enter their chambers. It was Abraham Lincoln's favorite.*

"Where there is no vision,
the people shall perish."

Proverbs 28:19

---

* For centuries, stonemasons have chiseled these words on the façades of government buildings, even though in many of them, the name of God cannot even be officially invoked!

Vision guides us. It inspires. It leads, even through those tough times when our own personal maps can get jumbled. We have often heard successful people say that when they went through their toughest times, out of money, out of ideas and out of luck, it was their vision for the future that pulled them through. They stayed true to their vision, and the vision sustained them.

Of course, vision is a very personal thing. None of us sees the world in quite the same way as the person standing next to us. As we undertake the task of creating a Vision Statement for ourselves and for our family, it is helpful to keep that fact in mind.

In the spring of 2005, third-grader Natalie Haga was given a geography homework assignment. She was to draw a detailed map of her neighborhood, pinpointing streets, schools, retail businesses, and her own house. While Dad searched the bookcases for the ten-year old, dog-eared Oregon atlas, Natalie ignored his mumbling, went into his home office and typed www. maps.google.com on the computer. When the page opened, she typed in her street address, city and zip code, and watched as a detailed map popped up on the screen. Then, she selected 'satellite view' from the pull-down menu, and before her dad could shout, "Hey, I found the atlas," the nine-year-old was looking at a crisp color photo of her small town (pop. 7,000) taken from a geostationary satellite flying 23,000 miles above the earth.

By the time her father had thumbed through the atlas index and found the county map, she had printed out two close-up views of her neighborhood. In one picture, her dad's car could be clearly seen parked in front of their house.

Natalie, and others young enough to accept high-speed internet access as just another normal part of life, see the world much differently from their parents. Her father's vision of the physical world—in fact, the vision of every generation before hers going back thousands of years—was clouded by the limits of technology. For most people over the age of twenty-five, the image of the world they carry in their heads is still a flat-map, printed and bound, world atlas vision. The simple truth is that our perception of what lies around the corner, across the county, over the ocean—even out in outer space—is shaped and framed by the tools with which we use to look. Our ability to develop those perceptions, and ultimately to come to conclusions about the world around us, is influenced as much by the 'vehicles' (i.e., books, newspapers, TV news, lectures) that deliver the information to us as it is by the information itself.

With the maturing of a functional internet, many of our concepts of the world around us have been turned on their heads. Our ability to find out about, to visualize and to participate in events around the world has become virtually limitless.

The ability to perceive the world around us, and to develop a personal vision which encompasses our family, friends, community and work relationships, is one of our greatest capacities. Humans possess no greater power than that of being able to conceive and bring to fruition the visions that shape their destiny. This uniquely human ability enables the artist to create, the scientist to invent, and the businessperson to build. Vision is the fuel for the engine that has fired all human achievement since the dawn of time.

Without it? Navigating through life without a vision is a lot like spending eternity inside a stuffy, grey-walled elevator, listening to the same bland Muzak tunes over and over, while going up and down, again and again, without the elevator door ever opening.

Equally bad would be to discover, at the end of a long life, that the vision for which you had grown, nurtured and sacrificed, was the wrong one. Or, imagine going through life believing you were a failure, that nothing you had done would ever make a difference, even though you had always tried to do what was right—only to have your children and grandchildren end up celebrating the things you achieved that seemed of so little consequence to you.

Take the example of Fred Snowberger, a pharmacist who defied the rough and tumble economy of the Great Depression to open a desperately needed pharmacy in rural Oregon in the early 1930s. He went deeply into debt to purchase inventory, equipment, and furnishings. But despite his best efforts, he could not keep the business afloat. Less than a year after he opened his business, Fred was forced to declare bankruptcy.

For most people, that would be the end of the story. Bankruptcy is a cherished American 'privilege', in which millions of people find shelter every year. In fact, it would be fair to say that there is no longer any shame in bankruptcy. Borrow, spend, fall behind and be forgiven. It is almost a national pastime.

But not for Fred. From the moment his debt was discharged by the court, he set about to repay every cent. He went years without a car, walking to and from his job every day, rain or shine. His family grew much of their own food, made their own clothing, and used everything they had until it was plain worn out. Every month he made small payments on the debts which, by law and custom, he had no legal obligation to repay. Year after year he cut back, sacrificed, scraped and made do without.

It took decades to repay his debt. The most productive years of his life were devoted to that single cause. One day, Fred walked up to the door of the last man he owed, his final payment in his hand. There were tears in the man's eyes as he accepted Fred's money. What a lesson, for both their families.

Fred believed his life was a failure. Were people to judge him only on that ledger account, it probably was. But a failure as a man, a father, a role-model, a living example of values like integrity, honor, obligation or character? Not at all. His life was much more than successful; it was significant.

Fred's children, and his children's children, recall his example seven decades later. They speak about him in tones of great respect and reverence. His life-his example-will strengthen those who knew him for generations. Can you imagine the impact of Fred's life on his heirs? [1]

In Guided Discovery, you will identify and reflect on the values you learned from your family and other important people in your life. The purpose is to prepare you to create what may become the most important document in your life and the lives of your inheritors. That is your Vision Statement.

Most of us are familiar with business mission statements, which are designed to define a business and its core activities to employees and to the outside world. The mission statement exists now, in the present, and describes the business as it is—or at least as it hopes it is.

Your Vision Statement is quite different. It describes what is to come. Its purpose is to shine a bright beam of light down a straight path, a map to guide, inspire and instruct generations of your family. It is more than a family history and less than a legal contract. Your Vision Statement positions your family to act as a team in decision-making. At the same time it describes how family members can support and contribute to one another as individuals within that process. In helping generations of your family understand their heritage from the past, your Vision Statement provides a foundation for family unity in the future. By using the family's own values and traditions as its building blocks, your Vision Statement becomes a credible, unique and powerful resource that is truly 'owned' by each succeeding generation.

There is no correct form the statement must take, no rules of style or structure to which it has to adhere. The length of your statement will be a function of your own story and the guideposts you wish to communicate. Regardless of its length, however, your effective Vision Statement will be inspiring, memorable, compelling, and it will be focused on your family's values.

It is not a document designed to be packed away once written. To be effective, and to achieve its goal of becoming a living statement of your family's history, dreams, desires and objectives, it has to be shared with every member of your family. It will be the framework around which *Family Council* meetings (described later) will be structured.

The Vision Statement does not create a formal legal entity—but then neither did the Declaration of Independence. But these two documents have much in common. They each outline specific expectations, and a vision for a better future based on values. Of course, The Declaration of Independence was hardly a big hit when it was first written. Fifty-six men risked their lives and personal fortunes when they applied quill pen to parchment. Each man signed the document knowing that he could be sacrificing everything he owned as a price for the independent nation he desired. (In fact, five signers were captured by the British and brutally tortured as traitors. Nine fought in the War for Independence and died from wounds or from hardships they suffered. Two lost sons in the Continental Army. Another two had sons captured. At least a dozen of the fifty-six had their homes pillaged and burned. All for a vision that each believed was worth risking his life and fortune.)

None of the families who have gone through The Heritage Process have faced quite the same degree of loss or hardships as did the signers of the Declaration, of course. However, when you commit to write your Vision Statement and to engage in a serious discussion about it with your family, you will most certainly be called on to display the courage of your convictions. In part that is because the values you identify in Guided Discovery are tangible, structured, definable and permanent.

Concrete ideals like the values that will frame your statement are not particularly fashionable among many segments of twenty-first century western culture. They are often portrayed as outdated and politically incorrect by the media and in the halls of higher education. The social science of ethics, wherein values change according to the ebb and flow of social whims, has, for many, replaced the ideal of moral absolutes, which do not change.

When you construct your Vision Statement, you will look far beyond contemporary social or political mores. After all, values like faith in God are not subject to the currents of popular culture. Honesty has no room for gradations of black and white. Love is not conditional. If you identify a strong work ethic as one of the values you want to transmit to succeeding generations, you know darn well what you mean by the words 'hard' and 'work,' no matter how anyone else may define it.

When you place your vision for your family's future on a bedrock of solid values, you are taking an important stand. It is not a political position, or a social statement. It is an affirmation of a lifetime of lessons learned. It is an announcement to your family that the values that strengthened and guided you, as they guided the people who passed them to you, are worth passing on to your children, and theirs. Whether those values are politically correct or not is not an issue. They are yours. They work. Because of that, they merit the respect and serious consideration of everyone with whom you share your vision.

That will not happen automatically. When your Vision Statement is complete, it is your responsibility to communicate its importance, and your absolute commitment to its basic tenets to each and every member of your family and others who are important to you. As you can imagine, that may take some doing. Unless your family lives in a 1950s sitcom, there are sibling struggles, old relationship scars, estrangements and unresolved conflicts of all kinds in your immediate and extended family life.

The Vision Statement isn't supposed to wrap colored bandages around old wounds, or to magically extinguish intra-family conflict. What it can do is provide a common direction, a clear purpose and a shared basis of understanding for your family as it plans for the future. Creating your Vision Statement for your family may not resolve all of your old family issues. However, it will provide your children and grandchildren a powerful tool for family cooperation, personal fulfillment and—most importantly—for leaving a significant legacy of their own.

While there is no standard format that your Vision Statement must follow, most will include many of the following provisions:

The Purpose of This Statement

People who have gone through the process of Guided Discovery often say they appreciate what explorers feel like when they stand on the crest of a mountain range and look back across the hundreds of miles of trail they forged. Now, they can also look forward to the lands that lie ahead with renewed enthusiasm and hope. Your Vision Statement is the vehicle by which they will communicate a sense of past achievement, along with their determination to support, inspire, motivate and strengthen their families in the future.

You *must* understand where we have been, your Vision Statement says. You should appreciate what sustained us through the journey and recognize the role that the values we hold dear played in our accomplishments.

Our Family's Story and How We Built Our Wealth

If there were a museum that featured the history of your family, where the exhibits were based completely on the information your children and grandchildren have about you right now, what would those exhibits look like? For example, in the diorama (complete with life-like mannequins of you and the people most important in your life as you grew up) that depicts your journey to success, what would you see? Would you see yourself putting in those fourteen-hour days, living in a simple one-room apartment with homemade curtains, or driving across town to save a dime on a can of beans? Or, would the exhibits only show you as they see you today: successful, comfortable, seemingly without a care in the world?

Your family needs to know your complete story. How you struggled. When you failed. How—and why—you were able to hang in there, despite the hardships, in spite of the setbacks. They should understand what success has meant to you, and what it does not mean. In this section of your Vision Statement you have the great opportunity (and rare privilege) of telling your story to generations of your family. For many people, this is the heart of the entire Process.

Our Financial Objectives

Many people are surprised to learn that the Vision Statement seldom addresses concerns about taxes. As people create a vision for the future, the objectives they identify tend to focus on matters more close to the family and its well being, including health, quality education and opportunities for the family to spend time together. Having spent a great deal of time identifying the values that helped shape their success, people look for ways to align those values with financial objectives they believe will sustain and strengthen their children and grandchildren in meaningful ways. Personal comfort and financial security are important, and most people make that clear in their Statements. How that comfort and security will be achieved and sustained, however, is not a financial *objective*.

Parents often express the desire to ensure that their children have the ability to pursue goals in their own lives that are worthwhile. Philanthropy can play a major role here, both as a glue that can hold families together and as a vehicle to support the kinds of causes in which the family believes.

Our Estate Plan and the Role of Our Children in Using Their Inheritance to Pursue Our Vision and to Create a Vision of Their Own

Here, parents often reflect on the bedrock values that sustained them as they describe the basic design of the estate plan they have created. This section is not an asset distribution plan. The parents may share their hopes that their children and grandchildren will honor and carry on the values and traditions for which they lived, even as they develop a vision of their own. It is an elaboration on the near-universal statement by parents, "I just want my children to be happy." You probably have advice on how they can best pursue their own goals, while still honoring the values you share as a family.

Our Definition of Wealth and the Desired Effects of Our Children's Inheritance

How does your family define wealth? As a financial asset base or as a family that is strong and healthy first, and prosperous second? As a family that can afford any luxury it desires or one that recognizes its responsibility to its community and nation?

What has achieving wealth and success meant to you? What can money do in your children's lives? What kinds of things can money never accomplish? Many parents express their hope in this section that the material inheritance they leave will not turn their children away from the core values that will ultimately determine the fate of individuals or even the entire family.

Balancing Our Children's Outright Inheritance with Their Charitable Inheritance

In the course of The Guided Discovery Process, many parents come to recognize the power of philanthropy not only as a tool for improving the world around them, but also as a unifying force the whole family can rally around. Where the parents have identified a particular cause, or established a family foundation or other entity to manage their charitable inheritances, this section may urge the children to see their own philanthropic involvement as the greatest opportunity they will ever experience.

Family Mission Statement

It is important that your family understands and actively supports the tenets of the vision statement. The Family Mission Statement says: this is who we are, this is what we believe, this is how we hope the estate we built will be used to strengthen our family for generations.

Family Council

Many Vision Statements provide that all family matters that require family approval must be conducted at a Family Council. The Council can review and make decisions for the benefit of the entire family. Family Councils can meet as often as needed, but, they must meet at least once a year. (Don't think sterile office building and conference table. Think family reunion and picnic table. One of the stated aims of many Family Council meetings is also for the family to have fun!)

We have seen how the foundational step of Guided Discovery provides multi-generational planning and training designed to help you pass the values (like work, faith, etc.) which helped you to accumulate or maintain your money, along with your money, to future generations. Through these steps, you discover not just what you have, but about what you care. You look at how your legacy will affect your inheritors. You define that legacy and then determine how best to involve your heirs.

The end product of this process, your Vision Statement, now becomes the source of authority for creating the comprehensive financial and estate plans that will achieve your family's most important goals.

To make that happen, there is one more ingredient needed: a team of advisors who will work together to translate your vision statement into action.

THE HERITAGE PROCESS™

– STEP IV –

IMPLEMENTING YOUR VISION

Translating your vision for your family's future into plans that place family before fortune, thereby strengthening and preserving them both.

CHAPTER ELEVEN

Implementing Your Vision

Problems cannot be solved by the
same level of thinking that created them.

Albert Einstein

T he power of your Vision Statement as a resource to guide the nuts
and bolts process of constructing your plan and putting it into
place cannot be overestimated. That resource exists not only as a
guide to future generations of your family, but as a guide to current–and
future–advisors. You have reviewed, identified, and articulated your values,
and crafted a vision for the future. Now, it is time to assemble the team of
advisors who will make it come to life.

Most folks who go through the Process already have trusted advisors in
place. You may have been introduced to a Heritage advisor by your CPA,
estate planning attorney, non-profit officer, or friends who have experienced
the Process for themselves. Those existing advisors will play an important
part in transforming the vision that has been developed under the guidance
of The Heritage advisor into concrete planning that will achieve your family's
goals across generations.

To get your plan organized and implemented with focus, energy and
efficiency, it is important that each one of your advisors understands that

there are two immutable positions around which all of your planning will flow:

1. Your children have already received their inheritance.
Your money is to be regarded as a tool, not as a legacy. That tool is intended to bind the family together, and to promote family unity, individual achievement, and community involvement.

2. The money is not to get in the way of your children's inheritance.
To put it succinctly, the tail is not to wag the dog. No provision of your plan is to put fortune before family.

This part of The Heritage Process will look differently than what you may be used to, largely because of the close collaboration of the advisors working on your behalf. In traditional estate planning, the attorneys, CPAs and brokers who represent your interests usually pass documents back and forth by courier or e-mail. There is no real collaboration. There is no road map based on your long-term family goals. What often happens in traditional planning is that advisors select pre-packaged *'product-solutions'* made up of investments and tax-saving strategies designed to accomplish one central objective: to pass as many assets as possible, with as little tax bite as possible, to the inheritors.

That kind of planning doesn't require a team committed to the long-term health and prosperity of your family. It is usually done by a collection of individuals working from a 'one-size-fits-all' playbook. The attorney selects documents A,B, and C from his Practice Forms CD, and fills in the blanks. His recommendations are e-mailed to the CPA and broker for the best tax reduction products they have. Mix in FedEx and a couple of faxes, and, presto–a traditional estate plan is born.

To be fair to the legal and financial professionals who have done planning for affluent families for the past one hundred years, we need to point out that tax reduction and asset distribution have been virtually the only things for which their clients ask. And, when it comes to those objectives, most advisors have done a good job. Consider what they are up against, including federal and state tax codes that are so complex that the government officials who write and maintain them admit even *they* aren't sure exactly what the regulations and administrative rules mean. According to the National Tax Limitation Foundation:

- In the 1930s, the federal tax system had only five hundred pages of laws and regulations and only sixteen pages on the income tax. Today the tax code is 45,622 pages long.

- Since the 1970s, the tax code has more than doubled in length.

- The tax code was altered seven thousand times between 1986 and 2001. (That explains the far-away look in your tax professional's eyes—who could keep up?) [1]

Add to that securities laws so murky and arcane that brokers begin and end every sentence to their clients with qualifications or explanations: *"This could be a good product for you, under certain circumstances, at least within parameter models we believe might have at least some application to your situation, or situations like yours."*

As for the purely legal aspects of traditional planning, take pity on the estate attorney who is forced to use the words *"maybe," "perhaps,"* or *"on the other hand"* in response to any question their client may have related to planning. (Ronald Reagan is said to have once asked his Chief of Staff to hire a legal advisor who was missing one hand. " A one-handed attorney," said the Chief of Staff. "Whatever for?" "I'll tell you why," said the exasperated President. "Every time I ask a lawyer for advice he'll give me an answer, and then raise one hand and say, 'But, on the other hand...'"

The issue is not the competence of the professionals who develop and implement traditional plans for people. Most have represented the purely financial and tax side of their client's planning quite well—especially given the byzantine maze of laws and regulations they must observe. Traditional planning does a good job of transferring assets while minimizing the tax bite.

But, we know that traditional planning alone cannot accomplish the most important legacy people wish to leave their loved ones: a clear vision for the future powered by values dedicated to the long term health–and prosperity– of the family. That goal cannot be achieved by individual professionals–no matter how good they may be.

Advisors who only work in traditional planning aren't flawed; they just haven't had the benefit of the fuller picture that Heritage Process planning provides. They work in virtual isolation. They focus on asset transfer and taxes because that's what their clients think they want. The true wealth–and health–of the families they serve (the multi-generation 'big-picture') has not been their focus because until the development of The Heritage Process there was not a credible, proven, professional practice model for them to follow.

For your Vision Statement to become translated into the legal and financial products and documents designed to accomplish your objectives, professional advisors from different disciplines have to turn to a new model of cooperation. They must truly work as a team.

However, the idea–and the practice–of *real* team planning and implementation is a difficult one for some professionals to accept. By true team planning, we mean a situation in which the legal / financial advisors to one client set aside any sense of competition to be your *'one trusted advisor,'* and instead align their talents and energies with others to form a high-performance team dedicated to achieving your objectives.

Legendary baseball manager Casey Stengel said, " *Gettin' good players is easy. Gettin' 'em to play together is the hard part.*" [2] Let's face it; successful advisors don't achieve elevated status in their professions without being smart. And tough. Some are even rumored to have egos that wouldn't fit inside the Grand Canyon. For the attorney or CPA who has always worked pretty much as a solo act, the idea of this level of team collaboration may take some getting used to. But the team approach will ultimately strengthen advisors as much as it does the families they serve.

The good news is that the failure of traditional planning to even face–let alone resolve-the host of problems that destroys so many families is no longer a secret. Thousands of families have experienced The Heritage Process, meaning there have been thousands of advisors who have, to one degree or another, also experienced the values-based legacy planning process for themselves.

With your Guided Discovery accomplished, your Vision Statement articulated, and your planning underway, it's time to meet with your family—and share the experience.

— STEP V —

INITIAL FAMILY RETREAT

*The first annual family event where family business mixes with fun,
solidifying the family's commitment to its vision and its values.*

CHAPTER TWELVE

The Initial Family Retreat

In every conceivable manner, the family
is the link to our past, and bridge to our future
Alex Haley

If you don't believe in ghosts, you've never been to a family reunion.
Anon.

What kind of images swirl in your mind when we ask this question: if you were to visualize your children and their spouses, (and grandchildren if you have them), plus your spouse, and perhaps even your brothers and sisters, all meeting in the same room–at the same time–to discuss the future of your family and your assets, what would that vision be like? Fingernails grating slowly down a chalkboard? The voice of a physician preparing you for an injection of a strong sedative?

One person told us he had a vision from the Cold War, when, in October, 1960, Soviet leader Nikita Kruschev wasn't getting the attention he felt he deserved from delegates at the United Nations General Assembly. So, the *'burly peasant'* (as the few Russian critics who hadn't been shipped off to Siberia called him) pulled off one of his shoes and began to pound it against the podium. Not a bad way to get the attention of world leaders more accustomed to the hushed, muted double-talk of diplomacy. (The fact that Kruschev was known to down a pint of vodka before he spoke in public, combined with the fact he also had absolute control of the second largest nuclear arsenal on the planet probably helped focus their attention as much as the shoe and the shouting.)

Your idea of what a gathering of your own extended family would be like may not be so dramatic. In fact, your family might be able to pull off a day long discussion of values, vision, money and the future of the family without a hitch. But, when families and their baggage (in this case their history and emotions, not their clothing and toiletries), complete with children and stepchildren (maybe even an ex-spouse), and siblings who might not have spoken to each other in years come together in common cause (money being first and foremost on some minds), the image of the raucous Soviet premier might actually be too mild for what you envision.

This may not seem to be the most uplifting or promising way to introduce the Initial Family Retreat, which is the next step in The Heritage Process. But, the Process is not an abstract philosophical ideal. It was designed to work in the real world. And in the real world, each family has a unique and often turbulent history, filled with equal measures of joy and accomplishment, sorrow and pain.

We call the Initial Family Retreat a "pre-inheritance" experience. It will be a forum conducted through adult-to-adult communication, perhaps a first in your family experience.

At the retreat, the focus is on:

- establishing communication among family members
- confirming that the children's 'real' inheritance has already been received
- organizing a family structure for unity
- passing leadership to the next generation
- preparing heirs to receive valuables without deteriorating their values

No one part of the Process will bring the history of your family to the surface like the Family Retreat. But the purpose of the retreat is not to tramp over old ground, or to heal the rips that mark the fabric of every family quilt. That is beyond the scope of any formal process. In fact, many would argue that it is in the furnace of trials and upheavals that brings families the greatest grief that the real strength of the family is forged. That is a question for philosophers and theologians. What we believe is this:

Other things may change around us, but we start and end with family.

Parents who have made the journey through Guided Discovery and on to the creation of their Vision Statement are usually anxious to hold the first Family Retreat. Anxious to share the vision, anxious to communicate the role for each family member, and, no doubt, just a little anxious about the event, period.

The retreat can be held at a hotel, conference center, family vacation home, destination resort, lodge–anywhere the family will have the opportunity to work together in comfortable surroundings. (Fun, by the way, will be added to the mix with the annual Ongoing Family Retreat we will discuss next.)

Some parents simply call their children, grandchildren, siblings or others who they want to attend. Others prepare and mail invitations. And, sometimes, the advisor who coordinates the retreat does the inviting for the parents. However family members are invited, the idea for the retreat is the same: to provide an opportunity to strengthen family commitments, implement a family council structure, broaden the family leadership base, and pass on family values.

Together with the Heritage-trained advisor, the parents will:

- Introduce family members to the Guided Discovery process through exercises the children and others (children's spouses, for example) in attendance will complete

- Share the family's story and how they accumulated their wealth

- 'Unveil' the Family Vision Statement

- Formally organize the Family Council

- Assess the family's human capital

- Facilitate adult-to-adult communication between the parents and adult children.

On the day of the retreat, the Heritage advisor begins the gathering with introductions and a discussion of the day's agenda. Then, the ground rules for the Guided Discovery questionnaires which the children (and possibly grandchildren) will complete are discussed. Ground rules are an important part of what happens during the retreat. This is not the time or place for a *Jerry Springer*-like free-for-all. The discussion sessions and interview events are facilitated by the advisor in an atmosphere of trust and respect. Everyone's comments (with individuals speaking one at a time) receive a respectful airing. Differing opinions and observations are not judged or criticized. The advisor keeps the family moving along the agenda, but in such a way as to provide a secure and productive environment within which family members can participate fully and honestly.

After the completion of the questionnaires, the advisor conducts a group interview with the children, often with their spouses present. Then, what is often the most powerful, poignant part of the retreat takes place. This is when the parents tell their story and how they or their ancestors accumulated the family's wealth. For many families—most, in fact—this is the first time that the children and grandchildren have heard the story in such detail.

Without theatrics or props, Mom and Dad simply sit down in front of their children (and grandchildren) and tell their story. Since the majority of affluent people earned their money the old-fashioned way—through hard work and ferocious personal determination, these stories almost always contain elements that surprise the listeners.

It can be difficult for young adults or teenage children who have known nothing but the privileged life of upper middle class or wealthy America to comprehend when their Mom starts talking about sewing patches on Dad's work jeans ("Dad wore jeans? Dad got his hands dirty?"), or picking fruit to can for the lean winter. Tales of one room apartments, cars that should have been going to the junkyard but had to be kept alive for one more month, early business failures, banks refusing loans, partnerships that crumbled—and sacrifice after hardscrabble sacrifice—often bring the toughest businessmen to tears, and almost always leave their children with a new measure of respect for their parents.

"I had no idea it was that hard for them," is the most common observation Heritage advisors hear from children and grandchildren after they hear the full story of how their parent's accumulated their wealth. It is a milepost in the family's history for the children—and for their parents. None of the accessories of affluence, from homes to cars, will ever look quite the same again.

Later in the day, the parents will build on the foundation they began to lay with their story of wealth accumulation by sharing their Vision Statement with the family. Now, their children can connect the dots from the values that sustained the parents through the hard times and kept them balanced through their success to the hopes and dreams the parents have for the family in the future. They will understand why the parents feel so strongly that the material assets they will leave are intended to support the real inheritance they have already given to their children.

Where there are old scars in families, old divisions, this is the time, in the natural progression from discovery to vision, that deeper understandings are often reached among family members. That doesn't mean miraculous healings of family wounds will happen, although Heritage advisors have seen families make tremendous strides in that direction. But, common ground is often established. Motives are better understood. Family history comes into clearer focus. Any or all of these can only strengthen a family's future, no matter the ghosts of its past.

The vehicle for the discussion and management of family business defined in the Family Vision Statement will come together through the work of a newly established *Family Council*. Now, unlike the United Nations Council (where shoe-whacking, political posturing and an occasional resolution approving the bombing of some remote desert chieftain's hideout is the order of business), the Family Council is charged as follows:

The Family Council is a forum where all family
members participate in activities and experiences to promote
family unity, family values and family traditions.

Fun, education and business, all accomplished within a context in which:

- What the family says in the room stays in the room, unless everybody agrees otherwise

- The welfare and harmony of the family is the most important consideration

- Only one family member talks at a time, and everyone is given an opportunity to speak

- Each person is encouraged to keep an open mind

- Blame and attacks are not allowed, and all individuals are free to talk about what they think and how they feel

As the idea of a council begins to take shape, it's a great time to discuss what each family member brings to the table. In total, this is your family's *human capital*. From the oldest attending to the little ones in the nursery next door, your family's human capital is comprised of its collective knowledge, talents, experience, values, skills, judgment and potential. The repository of possibility in the room with your family is limitless. When all of that pent-up capability is channeled with positive, can-do energy into the activities of the Family Council, well, Premier Kruschev would be well-advised to put his shoe back on and quietly leave the hall.

The organization and establishment of the council (complete with gavel, charter documents, record books, etc.) begins with the selection of a family council chairperson, who will begin the meeting with an open discussion to solicit ideas and make assignments of family members to handle the responsibilities of the council. For lots of folks, this is the first time they have participated in a structured meeting of this kind. Doing it with family makes it that much more challenging.

The Family Council is as effective and will be as enduring, as the goodwill and honest intent of the family members who participate in it; no more, no less. The importance and respect it will be accorded will be equal to the faith and hard work that go into maintaining, updating and communicating its message of family unity, from one generation to the next. That's why things like a formal meeting structure and leather-bound family record portfolio become important, visible symbols of the personal commitment made by each of the family members.

The chairman of Coca-Cola once said, *"If every truck, warehouse and bottling plant we own burned to the ground tonight, and if every bottle and can of Coke on store shelves in the world was emptied in the fight to put out the fires, it would not diminish the value of our company by one cent. The value of our company lies in the hearts, minds and intentions of our employees, and in the goodwill we have built with our customers over the years."* [1]

Families are a lot like that. Most families are ultimately stronger than any squabbles or disagreements that could tear them apart. At the Initial Family Retreat, you will discover that the ties that bind are far more important than any lingering emotional scars. Your family's worth lies not in its possessions. No inventory of assets and no balance sheet can measure the power of a mother's love, the potential of a child's mind, the generosity of a grandparent's heart, or the power of a father's values when they are applied towards a common goal.

When a family is willing to commit to a shared vision based on its own unique values, miracles can happen.

− STEP VI −

ONGOING FAMILY RETREATS

*An annual family event where family business mixes with fun,
which continues to solidify the family's commitment to its
vision and its values.*

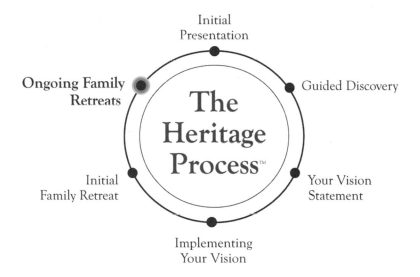

CHAPTER THIRTEEN

Ongoing Family Retreats

Some of our best memories exist only as 'freeze-frame' images. That's especially true of the paintings and drawings that illustrated the books we loved when we were children. The colors in those scenes seem brighter than those outside our offices windows today. That's probably the effect of a trick played on young brains which were not yet cluttered by politics, and work and the thousand distractions of everyday adult life. For us, some of the most magnificent and memorable images of childhood came courtesy of the great painter and illustrator, N.C. Wyeth, who single-handedly defined what classic adventure looked like for generations of American children.

In his illustrations for James Fenimore Cooper's *Last of the Mohicans*, clear-eyed frontiersmen battled brave Indian warriors in scenes splashed with mythical power. He brought *Robin Hood* and his unerring archery alive with astonishing energy and bravado, and he sent shivers down our backs with his dark and menacing portraits of pirate captains in *Treasure Island*. Fantastic images, vibrant colors, adventure on the grandest scale. That was N.C. Wyeth.

He painted many more kinds of scenes, of course. But none of his famous landscapes or portraits held our attention or remained so fresh in our memories as his super-charged adventures illustrations. Until now.

In 1941, Wyeth painted a simple country scene. It is set in the rolling foothills of the Adirondack Mountains, near dusk, on a clear autumn day. The central figure is an elderly man, dressed simply in a plaid shirt, canvas jacket and corduroy trousers. He is tall, with broad shoulders, a shock of white hair set above a handsome face bronzed by years spent outdoors. He is leaning over the top rail of a split-rail fence, his hands clasped around the bowl of a pipe. At his side, a black Labrador waits patiently for a command. Behind him, kindling smoke is beginning to drift above the cabin, where we can just make out the outlines of the man's wife through the curtain.

He is watching the car (a Woody station wagon) that pulled away from his cabin a moment earlier. It drove out and around the drive, turned left down the gravel hill, and is just passing below his vantage point. A man extends one hand out the driver's side, waving goodbye. From the rear passenger window, two young faces look up at Grandpa, their hands pressed against the windows.

Wyeth is a master of landscapes, so we expect to see the blended purples and greens and blues in the canopy of trees that cover the hills around the cabin. The softening afternoon light coming though the scattered clouds bathes the scene a blue-gold halo, but that, too is not what captured our attention after all these years.

What is so remarkable about this painting is not the setting. It is the expression on the old man's face. It's not what we would expect it to be. He is not smiling. He isn't returning his son's wave or giving a thumbs-up to his grandchildren.

In fact, his countenance is almost solemn. There is resolve in his eyes, a steely determination that has not been slowed by age. His head is erect, his gaze focused. Were he forty years younger, we would say that this was the face of an officer who was about to lead his troops into battle. Confidence without pride, conviction without arrogance, faith without reservation. This is a man who has thoughtfully and confidently made a decision of great consequence. Since we are watching his family drive away from his home, we can assume it is a decision about them.

It is true that we often see only what we set out to find when we look at paintings. As the years pass, however, we look with eyes that, having seen just about everything life can throw at us, don't tend to miss much. In this painting by N.C. Wyeth, we think we see just what the artist intended. His genius is his ability to transmit great meaning with just a few strokes of his brush. Complex effect from simple construction.

For us, this painting mirrors what we have seen in the faces of parents and grandparents during, and especially after, a Heritage Process family retreat. Tough to quantify, of course, and all but impossible to define with scientific precision. Just like a family.

At the conclusion of the Initial Family retreat, plans are made for the first Ongoing Family Retreat. If you have established a family council, created family committees and 'assigned' other family business, the next meeting might be held in less than a year. Typically, Ongoing Family Retreats are held at least annually.

This retreat has three functions:

- Family fun

- Family education

- Family business

The 'fun' part is important—just as important as any of the family business you may conduct. Remember, you may have all kinds of people attending, including extended family, kids and grandkids, spouses...so, make sure there are plenty of activities lined up for everyone.

The educational component of the retreat is a reflection of the goals and objectives your family began to set at the first retreat. They might include instruction by the parents or grandparents on the ins and outs of their businesses (if the family owns one). Reports by committee members on philanthropic organizations, family bank activities, group investment plans, etc. Outside resources, including family counselors and other advisors who can help with team-building or family communication, may also be included at the retreat.

When it comes to conducting family business, the guidelines for the way meetings will be managed may have been set up in advance. Also, the agendas, including the purpose of the meeting, the topics and the lead person for each topic, may also be pre-arranged. As much as possible, firm timetables should be set up for the meetings, and kept! (Remember: Frisbees and potato salad await.) Part of that involves agreeing on ground rules for things like cell phones and taking breaks. It is also helpful to decide who will lead the meeting, who will take notes, keep time, and who will act as 'traffic cop.'

Whatever the agenda, or upon what organizational procedures your family settles, there are some issues most family retreats face in common. These retreats are, as we said earlier, a 'pre-inheritance' experience. Adult children will become aware of how they view their money. That is an important concept, and no two families share those views in common.

We often remind people that every child grows up in a different family. That's why there is no one-size-fits-all template for the family retreat and no prepared list of specific outcomes your family should anticipate.

Whatever family business is conducted at the ongoing retreat, and whatever projects are brainstormed for future consideration, some traditions should be carefully nurtured and maintained. For example, the stories of grandparents, parents and others who have struggled, built, succeeded and just plain 'hung in there,' should be given a place of honor in the proceedings. These oral histories (which many families decide to videotape) quickly become treasured heirlooms.

Let us give you an example. This is a true story, one which illustrates how powerful and enduring the impact of the retreat can be for generations of a family.

The Danosevic family recently held its first ongoing family retreat. Nearly thirty family members flew and drove from around the country and gathered at a resort near the Sawtooth Mountains in Idaho. The father, Milos, is a successful fifty-four year old manufacturer who had been guided through the Process with his wife by a Heritage advisor the previous year. His two brothers and their children, plus assorted grandchildren, rounded up the family group. Only his older sister was absent.

Also in attendance (for the first time) was Milos' eighty-six year old father Dave and his wife, who had immigrated to the United States from Hungary in

1957. Dave was something of a legend and an enigma to his grandchildren, and, to a degree, even to his own sons. He owned and still managed a thriving lumber mill in Georgia, where he regularly put in ten-hour days. He had loaned Milos the money for his own start up, and was somewhat infamous for the way he had forced Milos to keep to his loan repayment schedule even when times were tough for Milos and his own family. "First you pay me," Dave was famous for saying, "then we can talk about your family."

His own grandchildren found Dave brusque, demanding, critical and deeply suspicious. He was also extremely sensitive to anyone getting physically close to him, and, so far as anyone knew, he had never shown any kind of physical affection to any human other than his wife.

Milos had worked on his father for months to agree to come to the family retreat. He worked even harder to get the old man to agree to sit down and tell his story to the assembled family.

On the second day of the retreat, right after lunch, Milos' extended family gathered in the great room of the rented lodge. Dave and his wife sat on plain wooden chairs in front of the fireplace, quiet, hands folded in their laps, deep in thought. Milos had never seen his father look so uncomfortable. It didn't help that Milos had been forced to threaten his teenage children with virtual banishment (no TV, Internet, or ipod...for the duration) if they did not attend. They sat, glum and sullen as only teenagers can be, anxious to get this unpleasant bit of family baloney out of the way.

When everyone was settled, on chairs, sofas, even on the floor, Milos went to the back of the room and switched on the video camera. His father raised his head a moment, and glared, but didn't speak.

"All-right, papa," Milos said quietly. "We're all here. Please...tell us your story."

The old man sat silently for a moment. Stiffly. People used to describe him as looking like a fire hydrant with a bad haircut. Those who had seen the octogenarian load stacks of pressure-treated 6" x 6" timbers in the back of customer's pick-ups faster than his twenty-year old employees just called him amazing.

Finally, Dave raised his head and looked out at the room filled with his offspring. "And, what is it you want to know then," he asked.

"Just tell us, papa," Milos replied. "Tell us how you came to America. "

"Come on Grandpa," chimed in one of the teenagers, "tell us why you wear the same suit every single day." The children laughed. That was a family joke. Rich Granddad wore the same clothes, day in and day out. Every day. Every year. What was that all about?

The old man did not rise to the challenge. Instead, he looked at the teenager and asked, "What did you have for breakfast this morning?"

"Geez, I don't know," she said, "maybe some yogurt, some toast, oh, and a latte."

The other grandchildren giggled. But only for a moment. When Dave spoke next, the room grew quiet. It stayed quiet for the next two hours as he talked. No one left the room. No one so much as whispered. They just listened.

As he began to talk, Dave stood, removed his jacket, and rolled up one shirtsleeve. None of his grandchildren had ever seen him without a jacket. His own sons couldn't remember the last time they had seen him with short sleeves.

"897631," Dave said in a whisper. He turned his arm palm-up, and extended it so his family could see the crudely tattooed numbers etched into his arm. "That was my number–my name actually–in the camps. Bergen-Belsen, Theresienstadt, and Auschwitz. 897631."

He put his other hand on his wife's shoulder. She was deep in her own memories. A few tears rolled down her cheek.

Dave told his story in a simple, matter of fact manner. In 1943, he was a young Hungarian Jew, an entrepreneur with interests in several Budapest businesses. He was married and father to a six-year-old girl. They were among the first Hungarians to be rounded up and packed into cattle cars by the Nazis. Their destination: Auschwitz.

He and his family were off-loaded in the vast field outside the main camp at dawn. It was freezing. Dave's wife and daughter were immediately separated from him. They quickly disappeared into the crush of thousands of Jews being processed for disposition to labor barracks, readied for transport to other camps, or, as in the case of many, directly to the gas chambers.

"I knew I would never see them again," Dave told his family. He looked at the granddaughter he had questioned about breakfast and said, "We had sour bread and weak soup for breakfast that day, on the train. The soup was served in the same tin containers we had used the night before as toilets. So, now I remember what I have for breakfast everyday."

Dave described how he was made boss of a construction gang because he had some carpentry experience in Hungary. He told of the sleep deprivation, the meager rations, the indiscriminate murder by guards. "I worked," he said, "I kept my head down, I worked longer and harder and better than anyone on the crew. I kept my job. I let myself hope. I prayed. I waited."

After a year, he was transferred to another camp and then another. Skilled managers like him were in short supply. In the two years he spent in the camps he was beaten repeatedly, he lost three fingers to frostbite, and the only friend he made in the camps died of cholera.

"I saw people shot because they bent down to pick up a potato-peel," he said, "SS guards drowned an old man in a fifty-gallon drum we had to use as a lavatory for their amusement. He had done nothing to them. And so I waited, I worked, I hoped against hope, and I continued to pray."

Two hours had passed since Dave began his story. His wife had not moved or said a word. The grandchildren had slowly, almost without thinking, moved together in a tight circle. Several were holding hands. This is not what any of them had expected when they came to this retreat.

Dave continued his story. One morning in April 1945, he and the other prisoners awoke to find that the camp guards had fled during the night. The surviving prisoners gathered in the roll-call yard, shivering, hungry, uncertain what to do. The day passed and then another. They made do with what they could, scavenging for food and bits of clothing. They also buried hundreds of prisoners whose bodies littered the camp grounds. They stayed put, mindful of the artillery shells bursting on the battlefield nearby.

At last, a patrol of American soldiers arrived at the camp and told them they were liberated. "They had no food for us, or medicine, or even instructions about where to go," Dave told his family. "So, we began to walk. Thousands of us, ragged urchins, without money or weapons or food. We lived off the land. We stole chickens, and ate roots. When the war ended a few weeks later, we thought we were home free. For a minute, I thought I could finally rely on someone else for a bit, let someone else take care of me. Hah!"

His laugh startled the family. "The war was over, but we were not free. I wandered for six months, eating when I could, sleeping where I could. I prayed and hoped, but I no longer knew what it was I was praying for."

Finally, Dave made his way to Vienna to the enormous train station set

141

up by American and British forces. It was a major repatriation center for millions of Europeans who had been displaced by the war. Dave registered with the authorities and got a boarding pass for a train that would finally take him home.

"I pushed my way through the crowds," he said," thousands of people, all trying to get home. But to what? For the first time since I was arrested and hauled off to the camps, I allowed myself the luxury of tears. I stood there on the platform, waiting for my train, in a crush of people as desperate and miserable as I was. I cried. I cried for my wife and my daughter, and I cried for my family and friends. I even cried for myself."

Dave's wife reached over and took both of his hands. She was sobbing now, her head buried on her breast. Dave's own eyes were moist, and tears flowed all around the room.

The old man took a deep breath and continued. "And then, well, it is almost beyond belief. The loudspeaker announced the arrival of my train. People swarmed onto the platform, everyone bumping against everyone else. It was madness. I was pushed backwards, and I stumbled over someone's suitcase. I scrambled to my feet, and I saw, and then I saw..."

Dave stopped. Tears were flowing freely down his face. He could not speak for a moment. Milos went up to him and hugged him. The grandkids held onto one another.

At last, Dave wiped his face with his one long sleeve, and said," I saw my wife. Standing right there in front of me. My wife! And next to her, my little girl, not so little any more. Right there on the platform, waiting for the train to Linz. My wife and my daughter."

He could not go on. Deep sobs racked the old man's body. His sons had never seen such emotion in their father. They had heard bits and pieces of his story, but never the whole thing, not in this detail. Wives cried. Grandchildren cried. But everyone wanted to hear the rest of the story.

Dave slowly calmed down, but it was his wife who picked up the story on the train station platform. "You see," she told her family," when we were separated from my husband at Auschwitz, we were processed, and asked if we had any special skills. I was a fine seamstress, and I told them I had owned my own shop. A lie, yes, but, in such a time God forgives, no? I told them my daughter's small hands were expert at working with fine laces, and that she was highly trained, too. We were given jobs, and soon we were moved to another camp. It was not easy," she said, "but we survived. So many did not."

The room was quiet. Finally, Milos suggested they all take a break. The teenagers who had been forced to come to the meeting were the most reluctant to leave their grandfather's side—even for a minute. So much made sense to them now. They understood his gruffness, his impatience, his attitude about work and prayer.

When everyone returned from the break, Milos announced that the story wasn't quite over yet. "Mamma and Papa didn't exactly waltz here from Hungary in 1957," he said. "Their adventure was only half over." Then, Dave told the second half of his remarkable tale.

He and his family returned to Hungary, only to find his businesses had vanished, and his savings along with them. He started a small construction company with two friends, and the little company thrived in the post-war construction boom. They had three sons, including Milos, and they began to enjoy a prosperous life. Then in 1956, disaster.

The Soviets invaded Hungary.

"In 1943, I was arrested for being a Jew," said Dave. "In 1956, I was arrested for being a capitalist!"

The new regime confiscated Dave's buildings and equipment and seized his bank accounts. Only hours before he was to surrender to police to face trial as an enemy of the people, Dave fled Hungary with his family. They made their way to Austria, and a year later, were helped out of the refuge camps and into the United States by a church in Georgia.

In America, Dave's credo of 'prayer, patience, work and hope' was put to the test once again. For the third time in his life, he applied himself, set goals, worked harder than anyone, and never looked back.

At least, not until this day.

His family was changed forever by the story Dave shared at the family retreat. His children and his grandchildren's grandchildren will continue to tell the story, for generations. Four simple values, faith, hope, patience and work, shine across the decades to illuminate the hearts of every member of

Dave's family. The values that carried him through some of history's darkest days won't simply be recalled, either. They have been enshrined by the family as the foundation stones for all of the business and philanthropy they do together. They even had an artist design a family crest emblazoned with Dave's values. It was used to make a family seal that is used to stamp every family council document they produce.

Dave's story is remarkable, and it is unique, but every family has its own stories of trials and triumphs. Sadly, most of those stories are never told. Their unvarnished lessons about the importance of values never get to their most important audiences, especially to the grandchildren.

At the Ongoing Family Retreat, The Heritage Process encourages and promotes the telling of these family histories. They are more than stories. They are treasures. The most valuable asset your family possess.

Chapter Fourteen

Family Philanthropy

We make a living by what we get,
but we make a life by what we give.

Winston Churchill

I t was the biggest box of chocolate you've ever seen," says Perry. "See's finest. Eight separate layers, each with, oh, at least thirty pieces of candy in each layer. Dark caramels, truffles drizzled with raspberry sauce, chocolate with little almond slivers, and those little bon-bon things. When I lugged it into the meeting room and plopped it on the table, twenty-five pairs of eyes lit up like it was Christmas. I didn't know attorneys and financial planners could drool like that!"

The setting was a Heritage Institute presentation for advisors to affluent families. Perry had just purchased the biggest, heaviest, and the greatest gift (or, depending on your viewpoint, the worst temptation) they could find in Chicago. (When he carted the massive box up to the See's candy counter and told the clerk that the twelve pound giant was for a business meeting, not for him personally, the *'I've seen-it-all-before'* salesperson just said, "Sure, fella.... whatever you say.")

At the presentation, Perry pulled the top off the large box, and slid it to the nearest person seated at the U-shaped conference table. "We want you to have as much of this candy as you'd like," he said. "But, you need to eat what ever you take right now, and we need to eat it up before we leave today." The combination of the words great chocolate, free, and all-you-can-eat didn't fall on deaf ears. As the massive container was pushed from person to person along the table, most took at least two pieces. For the next five minutes the only sounds in the room were the rustle of candy wrappers, an occasional "That is so good," and a few, "Did you try the ones with the pecans?"

When the box reached the far end of the room, and everyone had had their first shot at the candy, Rod picked up the box and carried it back to head of the line. "Okay, time for the second course," he said. And around the room the box went again. Most folks took just one piece this time, a few sighed, and waved it past (maybe with the just the slightest regret). The second trip around the room took only a couple of minutes. Once again, Rod carried it back to the other side, and urged folks to take their fill. Only a couple of hardy souls reached for thirds. The room grew quieter as confectioners sugar and cocoa powder began to work their sleepy magic on people who only twenty minutes earlier had greeted the arrival of the chocolate feast with loud approval.

"Well," said Perry when the box came to a complete stop, "we've only eaten the two top tiers. There are still six layers left. How about we send it around just one more time? Anybody up for that?" There were no takers. As good as the chocolate was, as infrequently as they may have had opportunities to indulge all they wanted, sometimes, enough is enough.

Just then, the door to the conference room opened, and a member of the hotel staff quietly entered. Her job was to check and refill the coffee and other refreshments on the table at the back of the room. Perry called out to her, "Excuse me, Miss—would you mind coming up here for a minute?"

She hesitated for a moment. Standing in front of a room filled with hotel guests at the conferences where she worked wasn't something she did. She approached Perry, and he asked her to turn with him to face the people at the table.

"Do you mind if I ask your name?" he said.

"I'm Magdalena," she replied, quietly, unsure about what it was they wanted to speak to her.

"Well, Magdalena," continued Perry, "I just wanted to take a minute and thank you for all you've done for us the past couple of days. You've kept the break table stocked, you've answered questions about the area for our folks, and you've been really pleasant and helpful. We appreciate that."

The twenty-five advisors gave her a round of applause. "Now," said Perry, "we'd also like you to have something, our way of saying thanks. Do you have children?"

"Yes," said Magdalena. "I have four, ages three to ten."

"Well, they're going to love this," replied Perry as he handed her the box of candy. "We had a few pieces ourselves, but I think there will be plenty for your children."

She took the (now just) ten pound box, her face beaming in a wide smile. The attorneys and financial advisors broke into applause again. Each one of them felt as if they had personally given her the candy.

Magdalena nodded to the group, thanked Perry and Rod, and left the room.

When she had gone, Perry turned to the group and asked, "So, which felt better? Seeing that wonderful candy come in here this morning and getting to eat every bit of it you wanted or watching Magdalena's face light up when we gave it to her to share with her kids? That's what an active program of philanthropy can do for the families you work with."

Philanthropy is a remarkable tool. It doesn't just cause people to feel good about themselves. It can strengthen, unite, and focus the energy of the family in ways nothing else can. For that reason, it is an important part of the values-based legacy planning process.

America has always been a nation of philanthropists. We give, in no small part, because we have been so blessed. A nation rich in natural resources and vast open spaces, with a population steeled by the melding of a hundred different cultures into one, the unique American character has much to offer. We are a people who not only understand abundance, but also the ways it can be put to use for the greater good of all people.

No nation gives the way America does. In 2003, charitable giving of all sorts totaled $241 billion, nearly two percent of the U.S. Gross Domestic

Product. In case you wonder how that compares to other industrialized nations, here are the world's biggest givers:

Nation	Philanthropic Contributions as % of GDP
• United States	2.00%
• Spain	0.8%
• Britain	0.6%
• Netherlands	0.4%
• France	0.2%
• Japan	0.1%
• Germany	0.1% [1]

A century ago, Andrew Carnegie and John D. Rockefeller spent fortunes establishing libraries, museums, universities and concert halls. Early philanthropists funded important medical research into disease prevention and cure, and even underwrote expeditions into the last uncharted wilderness areas on the globe. There was a strong religious component to much of this early philanthropy. The fantastic wealth of the great American tycoons often weighed heavy on their consciences.

Sheer wealth, however, is not one of the criteria for giving. When you combine American charitable giving with that other uniquely American tradition, volunteerism, you see that the instinct to share resources, including personal time, cuts across all economic boundaries. (It is interesting to note the point at which wealthy Americans become involved in giving. According to J.P. Morgan Private Bank, Americans seem to start giving 'serious' chunks of their money away once they are worth around twenty million dollars, whereas in other countries the threshold is around one hundred million dollars.) [2]

Earlier we cited a statistic from the Boston College of Social Welfare, which estimated that over the next four decades some forty-one trillion dollars will be transferred from one generation to the next. Paul Schervish, one of the authors of the study, estimates that as much as six trillion dollars of that transfer might be devoted to philanthropic purposes. Schervish also says there has been a fundamental shift in the motivation for giving:

"The rich used to give money only when they were scolded into it," he says. " Now they are increasingly giving out of a sense of doing something they want to do, that meets the needs of others, that they can do better than commercial interests, government or existing philanthropy. They can express gratitude for their wealth, and their identification with others less fortunate, and that makes them happy." [3]

One of the things that 'makes them happy' is the emerging consensus among advisors, counselors, non-profit organizations and affluent families themselves, that a family-based program of philanthropy is the most powerful tool there is for encouraging personal responsibility, accountability and family unity. Heritage advisors often hear parents say that their children never had a healthy appreciation of the power of money to do genuine good until they began to get involved in philanthropic activities.

What is so special about philanthropy? For one thing, it works on so many levels of human consciousness: for the nineteenth century robber-barons, charitable giving soothed religious guilt for having so much in a world where so many had so little. For others, supporting charity has meant getting plenty of ego strokes. Think Beverly Hills charity balls, paparazzi, and enough Botox to petrify a national forest.

Beyond guilt and ego, however, lie the deeper emotions, emotions that philanthropy also enhances. First, is the idea of personal significance. Pulitzer-Prize-winning author Ernest Becker said, "This is mankind's age-old dilemma; in death what man fears isn't extinction, but extinction without significance. Man wants to know that somehow his life has counted, that he's left a trace that has meaning. Its effects must remain alive in eternity in some way." [4]

Philanthropy does just that. Through it, people can experience the deeper significance about which Becker wrote. For families, that experience becomes exponential in its power and possibility. The trace you leave with your children through philanthropy can accumulate in their lives, and spread and multiply as it is passed to their children, and to their children's children, for generations. The disease of affluenza, which is caused by receiving money without meaning, can be cured by philanthropy, which makes money meaningful.

How does a family go about identifying and launching their philanthropic pursuits? These are key questions. First, we should be clear that the kind of philanthropy we're talking about is not necessarily the tried and true family foundation. What we really focus on in The Heritage Process is helping the family match its deeply held values with a concrete vision for the future in which all family members play an important role. All too often, traditional family foundations exist only in legal documents, coming to the surface for 'action' once or twice a year, usually around April fifteenth.

Our position is that affluenza can be avoided by teaching children a healthy, honest relationship with wealth. That lesson is often learned best through philanthropy. The idea will never take hold if they are simply handed copies of the family foundation annual report each January. This kind of education needs to be hands-on. Your children will benefit from the actual experience of researching non-profit organizations. Some families get this started by giving each of their children a small budget (say $1,000 per year—the amount really isn't important.) Before a child can make a donation to a cause, they must research it. Where does the organization get its funding? For what does it spend the money? What percentage of its budget goes for administrative costs, and what percent actually makes it 'on the ground?'

Management expert Peter Drucker said "Don't over fund projects—you'll ruin them." [5] He knew that the most successful businesses and the best ideas are born out of scarcity. Great concepts more often come from struggling entrepreneurs in garage workshops than from teams of highly paid consultants sipping lattes around polished conference tables.

The same principle can be applied to children: "Don't over fund children—you'll ruin them. It will impair their character and destroy their motivation to succeed."

When children study the plight of people in need, and they understand that they have the wherewithal to do something about it, it is a powerful experience. That is especially true of children who have never experienced scarcity in any respect. With knowledge about the needs of others, children can experience scarcity from the vantage point of the helping hand in the field. As one advisor put it, "Instead of merely sailing on a sea of riches, children can experience an ocean of needs."

When children are given a challenge and the means to do something about it, a whole host of positive decision-making skills will be put to use and honed. They may come to the conclusion (on their own!) that money alone can never solve the ills of the world, an observation which will enhance their maturity and put their own relationship with money in sharper focus. They can study and choose between dozens of charitable organizations and countless worthy causes 'competing' for their attention and their money, which will sharpen their discernment skills and help them understand that real life is filled with hard choices.

One parent told us a story about his thirteen-year-old daughter, Julia. She and her two brothers had each been given $1,500 and charged with researching at least three charities of their choice before reporting back to the family. Then they could send their checks.

A week before the meeting date, Julia had not started her research. Boys, cheerleading practice, her cell phone and the neighborhood mall took up most of her spare time. Finally, her parents had to give her an ultimatum: choose some groups to study, and prepare your report, or your four favorite activities would be out the door for a while.

"Yeah, well, fine," Julia pouted. "I guess I'll study about starving kids in Africa or something."

The next Saturday, the family sat at the kitchen table to listen to the charitable giving plans. Julia's sixteen-year-old brother Peter reported that he had just about been ready to select an organization that bought used farm equipment in the US and shipped it to Mexico as his preferred choice when, as he put it, 'he figured out' how to read their financial disclosure report.

"Do you know that they spend 78¢ of every dollar that people give them for salaries and administrative costs?' he said. "That is so bogus! Only 22¢ of every dollar they get actually goes to buy farm equipment.....if I gave them my $1,500, only about $300 would even go to the people who need it." So, he had found a smaller organization that relied on volunteers to deliver the equipment to rural Mexican farms.

"And they only need 18¢ of every donated dollar to do exactly the same thing. That is way cool."

Anthony, the eleven-year-old, had visited three animal shelters in neighboring communities. They all seemed to do a pretty good job, and they were all staffed by volunteers, but the one that caught his attention was about to do a direct mail campaign about spaying and neutering pets to every household in the county. "They had a sign on a bulletin board asking if people could help with the cost of printing and postage," he said. "They needed $5,000 in all, so I decided to give them half of my $1,500 and then to split the rest between the other two shelters. They both seemed like they had too many pets and not enough cages."

Now, it was Julia's turn. Her parents weren't sure what to expect; she hadn't exactly been a fireball of enthusiasm when it came to doing her research. So they were surprised by what they heard.

"I have decided to give my money to a foundation that trains teachers in equatorial Africa," Julia announced.

"But, honey," said her mother, 'we thought you were researching organizations that deliver food to hungry people? How did you go from that to helping to fund teacher training....you've told us that teachers are the lowest life forms on the planet!"

"Well," said Julia, "they still are, at least my teachers in America are. But when I started to study world hunger I discovered that about one thousand children die every hour of every day from starvation and preventable diseases, like measles and stuff. And I really wanted to just give my money to one of the groups that buy lots of food and send it to those places.

"But then I started to wonder, how come so many kids are dying from starvation in countries that have so much good farm land," she continued. "I mean, that doesn't make any sense. So I studied some more, and I talked to my geography teacher. After a while, I realized that the reason so many kids are dying isn't because they don't have enough food or clean water or medicine. It's that a lot of the leaders in those countries, and the people in power, are stealing so much from their own people, and fighting all the time, burning the farms and stuff like that. I just didn't think that sending over more food to those countries would do any good."

Julia's parents were quiet for a minute. This was their bracelet-jangling, gum-popping, ipod-blasting daughter? Their Julia was making these adult assessments, using this level of reasoning?

"I have to ask you," Julia's dad said at last. "How do you go from deciding not to give food to countries with corrupt governments, to deciding to give it to colleges that train teachers?"

"Oh, that's easy," Julia said. "I mean, if kids don't know anything, if they can't read and think for themselves, how will they ever change things? I guess if there are more teachers life will get better someday. I know it won't happen right away, but it's better than giving them some food that will just get stolen as soon as it gets there."

The next day, they family sat down together and wrote out checks for the organizations the children had researched. They also committed to doing the same thing the following year. For two parents, the power of philanthropy to bring a family together became very clear.

This is what can happen when parents give children a responsibility that matters, as opposed to another chore or a lecture. When children discover a passion on their own, when they learn they can make a difference, when they have the opportunity to come face to face with what poverty and scarcity really do to people, they can also begin to appreciate the proper role of money in their lives; as a tool to support the things that matter.

With The Heritage Process, family is at the center of every long-term financial decision that is made. Family banks, family council investment clubs, grandchildren investment clubs, newsletters, family scholarship funds–these are all examples of values-oriented projects that put family before fortune, and which, through the process of diligently maintaining that perspective, end up strengthening them both.

The power of philanthropy to unite families in common cause is extraordinary. It does not require great wealth; there is no relationship between the amount of money the child is given to donate to a worthy cause and the lifelong impact that the project can have on them. Five dollars can deliver the same result as five thousand: such as a child who learns empathy, decision-making, 'over-the-horizon' planning, problem solving–so many of the skills and attitudes necessary for a healthy (and happy) adult life.

If you have any doubts about the ways philanthropy can strengthen your own family, put it to this simple test...

Buy a twelve pound box of chocolates, and call everybody to the table....

PART IV

CHAPTER FIFTEEN

Meet the Walkers

Most affluent people earned their money the old-fashioned way: through hard work and personal sacrifice. Studies show that seventy-five percent of all affluent people (defined as having a net worth over three million) made it themselves.[1] No handouts, no winning lottery tickets, and no magic lamp with a genie inside.

These are folks who have built businesses from scratch when scratch was just a couple hundred bucks, an old warehouse and a powerful idea. They've done every job in the building, from cleaning the toilet to painting the walls. They know what it's like to struggle and pray and dig deep in their own pockets to make Friday payrolls—most have gone more months without pay themselves than they care to remember. In the early days they held off competitors, crooked suppliers and government bureaucrats with nothing more than grit and determination and hope.

All that to achieve success. All that to achieve their dreams, and to build a better life for their family than they ever had for themselves.

It's a tough pill for many successful folks to swallow when their own children or grandchildren fail to show the same motivation, drive or ambition they themselves display. Their lives are stories of single-minded focus and relentless pursuit of their dream. That makes it hard for them to understand why their kids get mixed up in drugs, why they can't keep a job, finish school or hold their marriage together.

When any family crumbles from the weight of these problems, parents ask themselves a lot of questions. Why us? Why can't the children understand how good they have it? Why have I worked so hard all these years, only to see my family in turmoil, and my business at risk of just fading away for lack of a family member capable of taking charge when I retire?

According to the 2003 survey of affluent Americans conducted by US Trust Bank, seventy-five percent of parents worry that their children's lives might be adversely affected by wealth. So, if you're a parent or grandparent who is facing any of these issues with your offspring, take some comfort in the fact that you are not alone. The truth is that affluenza is not only real, it's an epidemic.

The point of The Heritage Process is not to do a psychological or financial makeover of your family to make it look like the Cleavers on *Leave it to Beaver*. It's really about identifying the strengths (values) that have sustained your journey and enhanced your success, sharing them with your children / grandchildren, and then reaching a common vision, based on those values, for your family's future which all of you pledge to support.

It's true that there is no such thing as a 'normal' family. There are only 'real' families. (Our friend Joel Sonnenberg likes to point out that "everybody is normal—until you get to know them.") In our practices, we have met literally thousands of affluent families. While it's true that no two families are exactly alike, there are remarkable similarities among most of them when it comes to how their wealth affects relationships within the family. That fact, combined with the ninety percent inheritance plan failure rate, makes it clear that whether you value your money more than your family or your family more than your money, you're going to lose them both if you fail to address certain issues.

To see how the process works, and how it is different from traditional estate planning, let's follow a real family (names changed) through the Guided Discovery Process.

The Walkers, David and Sharon (both age fifty-nine), have three grown children, and assets of around nine million dollars. The manufacturing business Dave owns is cyclical in that they have a lot of money when they finish a custom job, but then may have little or no income while they prepare for the next one. During the '80s they made excellent returns on their cash reserves by investing them in the stock market (mostly in tech stocks, since that is with what they were familiar). Then, in 1999-2001, when the tech bubble burst, they lost a great deal of money in the market, depleting their working capital and almost ruining the company. Consequently, Dave has become a much more conservative investor.

Dave and Sharon signed their wills years ago. They call for the entire estate to go to the survivor at the first death, and for the estate to be divided equally between the three children at the death of the survivor of them. They have not updated their wills for several years although the value of the business has grown substantially since the setback in the stock market.

They are philanthropic at heart but not in practice. Dave gives to some charities in ways that will bring attention to his business. But, other than that, they are not involved. They would like to help more—particularly with a rehabilitation center that helped their daughter Mary and her teenage daughter Tiffany beat their drug/alcohol addictions. They also know how important it is for kids to have good role models and positive peer support (in part because their son Mark's kids are doing well), and so they would like to support organizations that help children—both with role models and positive peer involvement. They feel like they let Mary down by not making her go to college, and so they want to make sure all of their grandchildren have the opportunity to go to college or trade school.

Dave feels pretty good about the plans he has made for the future of his *money*. But from his own experience with his father and siblings, and the experiences of his own children, he knows that the strength of a balance sheet and the strength of a family are two very different things. He knows he needs to do more to plan for the future of his *family*.

Dave had heard about the emerging field of "values-based" estate planning. He liked the idea of planning for the future of his family first and letting the assets he had accumulated act as a tool to keep the family healthy. So, he went to a major brokerage to ask about their legacy-planning services, and they invited him and Sharon to a seminar.

At the seminar, they were told they could eliminate estate taxes by passing what they could to their children estate tax free, giving the balance to charity, and then buying life insurance to "make up" what they give to charity. Although he liked the idea of eliminating estate taxes, Dave had several problems with the concept:

1. He had no idea how large his estate would be when he dies,

2. He had no idea how much he can pass estate tax free when he dies, or if there would even be an estate tax, since that seems to change every year, and

3. He didn't want to buy any more life insurance

What Dave discovered is that for the most part the values-based legacy planning services offered by banks and brokerages equated estate tax reduction with strengthening values since, in their estimation, a family with more money would be stronger and healthier simply by virtue of having a fatter bank balance. And it goes without saying that these large institutions also just happened to sell the financial products to achieve that estate tax reduction 'right down the hall.'

At work, Dave likes to direct a sales rep's attention to a sign posted behind his desk:

"When your only tool is a hammer, every problem looks like a nail."

For him, the product-oriented solution offered by banks and brokers fell into the hammer and nail trap. He understood that products and plans would always constitute the purely financial component of his estate plan, but, he also knew that looking at financial products first as a way of keeping the family itself strong and healthy was a classic case of putting the cart before the horse.

His attorney told him about The Heritage Process, which doesn't promote products, and which works in collaboration with the client's existing advisor(s). Unlike the brokers and banks who offered a watered-down version of values-based legacy planning as a way to sell products, his attorney told him that Heritage concentrated on guiding the family to a shared family vision statement, in which the money is just a tool for achieving the family's more important goals.

Dave and Sharon decided to take a look at The Heritage Process. They asked their attorney to introduce them to a certified Heritage advisor. Here's their story, in their own words.

DAVE : I grew up in a pretty small town with my older brother and younger sister. My father had a small manufacturing outfit, my brother and I both worked for the company. Dad used to say that hard work spotlights the character of people: some turn up their sleeves, some turn up their noses, and some don't turn up at all. Even as a kid, I remember I was always building things, or taking things apart and re-building them. When our father died, he left the business to his three children, equally. My brother took over as president. Basically, I ran the plant, while my brother ran the office.

SHARON: When I met Dave, I was nineteen, working as an assistant bookkeeper in his father's business. He wanted to meet "the new girl with the dimples." We hit it off right away. I really liked his energy and his focus; he was more "serious" than the college boys I had been dating. He liked my optimism and how I could always make him laugh. Dave and I were married on the six-month anniversary of our first date. I continued to work for the company, but when Mary was born a couple of years later, we both felt it was important for our kids to have a "stay-at-home Mom."

DAVE: In the years after my dad died, things were not going smoothly between us kids. My sister thought my brother and I were both taking too much in salaries, and she should get more, even though she did not work for the company. My brother thought he should have a higher salary, since he was the president. I constantly had problems delivering the product because my brother allocated too much to salaries and dividends, and there was often insufficient capital to run the business. Compounding my frustration, my real passion was designing new things—not merely overseeing a production crew.

Finally, I couldn't take it any more and left the company to start my own business, a partnership—with the man who had been the controller of my father's business. After we left, the company went into a steady decline; eventually they sold all the equipment and closed the doors. Our new business has thrived. Unfortunately, my brother and sister blame me for the failure of our father's business, and we are no longer on speaking terms.

SHARON: Things were rough for Dave for a while. All that stress at work, and then the risk of striking out on his own. He worked eighty and ninety hours a week, building a successful company from the ground up. Talent and hard work proved out, but there were times in the early years, when Mary was young, that Dave wasn't "there for her" very often. Later, when the business was on a solid footing, Dave was able to do things like coach little league for our sons Mark and Shawn. I think he felt a little guilty, so he compensated for his lack of availability by buying gifts for Mary.

MARY (Age thirty-seven): I definitely wanted to be a Daddy's girl. With him being gone all the time, I did crave his attention. I'm not saying that's an excuse, but in high school I started hanging out with kind of the wrong crowd, drinkers and druggies. I crashed the car I was given for my sixteenth birthday. They were just glad I wasn't hurt and never realized I had been drinking. I was drunk at a party in my senior year when I got pregnant with Tiffany. The father agreed to marry me but it barely lasted a year. We were already separated and planning on getting a divorce when I got pregnant with Renee. That guy split, so the three of us moved back in with my parents until I could get on my feet.

SHARON: They were going to move back in "temporarily" until Mary could find a decent job. At first that was unlikely because she had never graduated high school. We made sure she got her GED and paid for her to take some business classes at the community college, but after three years she still wasn't "on her feet."

MARY: I met a really nice guy; he treated me well and loved my girls. We got married and moved in together. Unfortunately, alcohol soon became a problem for us both. Finally, because I was worried about my girls, I asked my folks if they would let the three of us move back in while I went through rehab. After I successfully completed the program, my dad loaned me $50,000 to help buy a house. It's a nice place with a fenced in yard for the girls. I do have a boyfriend who lives with us. I'm not too sure I'd ever be interested in trying marriage again.

DAVE: We didn't mind helping Mary when she needed it. Your first instinct as a parent is to do what you can to help your kids. Also, Sharon and I have a pretty close relationship with Tiffany and Renee. We love all our grandkids, but we're a little concerned for the girls. We consider ourselves pretty "modern," but neither Sharon nor I are very happy about Mary having her boyfriend live with her. And Tiffany started drinking herself when she was twelve—secretly, of course. She only just turned eighteen and she's already gone through rehab, which we paid for.

MARK (Age thirty-four): My sister has had a rough life. As the middle child, I think I tried hard to be the "good" one; my way of trying to earn attention. I've worked at my dad's company since I was sixteen and have steadily moved up the ladder. I'm right where I want to be right now, in terms of responsibility. Unlike my Dad, I am not a natural leader, so he and I have mutually agreed that, in the event of his death, I will not be taking control of the company. I am comfortable—pleased, in fact—with this arrangement, but my wife Denise resents it. She thinks because of all my years at the company it should be mine by "birthright." Denise and my folks don't get along too well. I think part of the reason is that Denise believes they favor Tiffany and Renee over our two boys.

SHAWN (Age thirty): I don't envy Mark. He seems to have found a place where he fits in life at our dad's company, but his wife seems determined not to let him enjoy it. I started in property management right out of college and now have a pretty successful real estate brokerage, so I don't face any pressure from my wife as far as inheritance goes. Mark and I are agreed: there may have been some favoritism toward Mary, but she needed the help. We know that if we had needed any help in a similar situation, our parents would have been there in a heartbeat. So there's no resentment between us kids.

SHARON: With what happened between Dave and his siblings, family unity is so important to him. The whole family always celebrates Thanksgiving and Christmas together, and we always plan a summer vacation where the whole family is invited. At least two out of the three kids are always able to come with their families.

For the Walkers, the 'next step' in their planning process was about to begin. Working with a Certified Wealth Consultant accredited by The Heritage Institute, they began to learn about The Heritage Process, and how it could help them beat the odds their own estate plans would fail. What the Walker family experienced in the first step *(Guided Discovery)* and how this process led them to a clear vision of what their family's most important goals and objectives were, is described in detail in the next chapter.

CHAPTER SIXTEEN

The Walkers in
Guided Discovery

These are highlights of one of the Guided Discovery conversations that the Walkers experienced with their Heritage advisor. Dave and Sharon were pretty clear about their personal, financial and business goals, and their family dynamics were not terribly complex. Even so, sometimes the advisor has to work diligently to draw fully developed answers from the participants. Not so much in terms of uncovering secrets, but to help participants get to a point where they can clearly acknowledge any important values and significant influences in their lives which may have gone previously unarticulated. (This is one of the reasons we remind potential participants, "The Heritage Process is not easy!")

Here is some of that conversation.

Heritage Advisor: Test, one, two... Okay, this is Asa Wiseman, Heritage advisor, and I'm here with Dave and Sharon Walker. Dave, Sharon, you understand the only reason for the tape is to make a transcription of our meeting today. When we are done, I will return the tape and my copies to you. These are for you, not me. What we say here remains confidential.

Dave: I understand.

Sharon: Yes.

Heritage Advisor: Okay, why don't we start right in. Dave, I see on your questionnaire that you list your paternal grandfather as a big influence on your life. Why is that?

Dave: Actually, I barely knew him; he died when I was seven or eight. I remember my older brother and I being slightly afraid of him because he was very exacting, and he spoke with a heavy accent. But my dad always talked about him. How he came over from Germany after World War I with a young bride. His name was Volker, it got changed to Walker at Ellis Island, which was great with Granddad. He wanted his kids to grow up as Americans; he really saw this country as the land of opportunity.

He was a skilled machinist, but he sold the few tools he had left after the war to pay for passage to the States. He worked two jobs for almost two years to save enough money to buy tools and open his own machine shop. Even as a machinist, he never made much money; he was more interested in the quality of the work than his profits. But he taught his skills, and his expectations for high quality workmanship to my dad. So when Dad started his manufacturing company, it quickly built an excellent reputation.

Granddad did have a more direct influence on me. Or maybe he was just the quickest to recognize where my innate abilities lay. He bought me my first Erector Set, when I was only four. I'm sure people told him that I was much too young for such a complex present, but I loved it. I took great care of it, and never lost a single nut or washer. Thirty some odd years later, when I realized none of my own kids were natural tinkerers, I sold it to a collector for a bundle!

Sharon: I never knew that you were already a tinkerer as a child. I always assumed your engineering and design skills were learned at your father's company.

Dave: I developed some skills, there, but I think I ended up as sort of a combination of my dad and granddad as far as mechanical abilities, and my mom for my creative side.

Mom was a stay-at-home housewife, as almost everyone was back then, but she had a great mind. She was always challenging us kids with puzzles and riddles, brainteasers. She was also quite a talented painter, we have some of her work hanging in our home. I hope our kids will honor their grandma's memory and share them after I am gone.

HA: Getting back to your granddad. You said that he was the most important influence in your life. That had to be from more than just an Erector set and secondhand stories from your father. When you hear the name Grandpa Walker, what thought jumps into your head?

Dave: It's funny you should say that because the thought that just jumped into my head was my little sister's fourth birthday. Granddad gave her this amazing toy calliope; it rolled on its own, powered by a big watch spring, and its little pipes sounded notes. He made it all from scratch out of plans in his head. And I remember my father saying, "Dad, that must have taken you hours and hours. She's only four; she would have been happy with something much simpler." And my granddad fixed each of us with a hard stare, and said in his thick accent, "If you're not going to giff a task your best effort, zen you are joost vasting your time."

My dad and all three of us kids remembered that. Even my sister in Home Ec classes in school, I remember her talking about Granddad, and how her sewing had to be exactly so many stitches per inch, exactly straight.

HA: You have drawn a pretty clear line through your mom and dad and to your granddad as the major influences in your life. Are there others?

Dave: I think probably next in importance would come my high school shop teacher. He was this amazing woodworker with only one arm. He didn't lose it in an industrial accident, he was wounded in Korea. That's all he would ever say when asked about it, "I was wounded in Korea." My dad was pretty good friends with the principal, though, and he told me that Mr. Panagapko got the Medal of Honor for saving what was left of his squad after they were ambushed. The students would sort of whisper about it amongst ourselves, but we were all too afraid to ask him about it.

It wasn't his heroics in the war, however, that influenced me. First of all, I had never seen somebody so able to command the respect of the students without yelling or raising his voice. Secondly, when he assigned class projects there was never just one right answer, one way to do things. He really encouraged creativity, taught us to examine problems from many different angles. The sign I have behind my desk, "When your only tool is a hammer, every problem looks like a nail" is a tribute to him. It was one of his favorite sayings.

HA: Can you describe what you learned from your family and mentors in just a few words?

Dave: Hard work, for sure. Also, high standards of workmanship, a quiet style of leadership, creativity and problem-solving.

HA: What else is important to you?

Dave: Family unity. Family harmony. After my Dad died and I became estranged from my brother and sister, I was determined to do everything I could to keep my family tight. That's one of the reasons I wanted to try this process. It wasn't us kids receiving equal shares of Dad's business that caused problems. It was that there was no succession plan. Furthermore, there was no plan at all for how the heirs might function as a whole, with the family's interests instead of individual issues paramount.

The Advisor went on to explore Sharon's family history, and the impact that her family's values had on Sharon and on her children.

The types of questions that Dave and Sharon Walker experienced in their Guided Discovery show how participants discover their own values based on their own experiences. The Walkers met with their Certified Wealth

Consultant two more times before they completed their Vision Statement.

Over a three-month period following, a team comprised of their CPA, attorney, Heritage advisor and an investment advisor worked in close collaboration to craft plans based on their Vision Statement. Then, the Walkers held their Initial Family Retreat, which they described as a powerful experience for the entire family.

Just before this book went to press, they held their first Ongoing Family Retreat.

CHAPTER SEVENTEEN

The Heritage Process and Your Family

Do you remember your great-great grandfather's
first name and what was important to him? Would you like your
great-great grandchildren to remember your first name
and what is important to you?

Whatever their individual approaches to estate planning may be, research and our combined experience show that most people share the same four primary goals:

1. They want to protect their family from ever being destitute.

2. They want to provide their family with opportunities that will help them mature into healthy, productive adults.

3. They do not want to promote a non-working lifestyle. As investor Warren Buffett said, *"The perfect inheritance is enough money so that they would feel they could do anything, but not so much that they could do nothing."*[1]

4.   They want to minimize conflict within the family.

Simple goals. Clear goals. Ones that come from the heart as much as from the brain. But where in the typical traditional estate plan can you point to the tools that will achieve those goals?   In the mounds of accounting and actuarial paperwork or in the binders stuffed to bursting with contracts, trust structures and contingency codicils?

Traditional planning, by definition, is concerned with one thing and one thing only: the transfer of assets.   It has no mechanisms for the transfer of values. Traditional planning is static; it   not only ignores the dynamic realities of family interaction, it doesn't even recognize that families are fluid organizations that change as constantly as the weather.

Traditional planning asks   "Who gets the money that's left over after taxes, legal fees and administrative costs are paid?"   The Heritage Process asks, "How can we develop a plan that will pass on the family's true wealth, its traditions, values, morals and virtues, using the material wealth of the family as a tool to secure those values for generations to come?"

Traditional planning counts the assets, and divides and distributes the 'spoils' according to the language of the Will. Heritage planning guides people to discover what they have, and about what they care, to understand how their legacy will affect their inheritors, to define the legacy they want to leave and to determine how they can leave a meaningful legacy and implement their vision statement.

People who create traditional estate plans focus on how much money each inheritor should receive. Those who craft their plans on a foundation of values reflect on what money has meant to them, and what meaning they want it to have for their children.

Through its unique values perspective, Heritage has redefined the whole idea of what planning should be. Or perhaps more accurately, Heritage has taken the idea of estate and financial planning back to what it is that people actually want to accomplish: using money as a tool to keep the family intact and healthy.   By putting family before fortune, and making a shared vision the foundation for all its plans, The Heritage Process has already helped generations of families:

- Accumulate and create wealth
- Watch it, and nurture its growth
- Protect their wealth
- Enjoy their wealth
- Transfer their wealth

Heritage planning is important. It opens family communication in new and meaningful ways as family members identify shared values and craft a unique family vision designed to achieve shared goals. It inoculates inheritors against affluenza, especially by virtue of the family's active support of and participation in philanthropic activities.

Through philanthropy, family members experience a reduction in the sense of separation from the world at large that people of wealth often experience. They come to view their money as a blessing that can benefit many people beyond their relatively small family unit, and they experience a greater sense of personal worth and self-esteem. Plus, the family that is involved in shared philanthropy projects creates a powerful forum for communication between generations and for practicing family democracy and power sharing. Best of all, as grandparents and parents watch their children manage increasing levels of responsibility with their philanthropic projects, it makes the task of 'letting go' in other areas of the family financial picture much easier for the older generation.

The foundation of The Heritage Process rests on memory and meaning. The memories you keep of your parents, grandparents, the ancestors who came before them and other important people in your life are far more important than many of us realize. They are, in a very real sense, a kind of emotional, intellectual and spiritual DNA that you inherit, whether you are conscious of it or not. In turn, you will pass this 'built-in' recipe for success or failure, happiness or despair, faith or hopelessness, to your own children and grandchildren.

Memory is more than emotion. From a psychological viewpoint, it is the actual fabric with which we weave our perceptions of ourselves and others. It is what we use to help determine how to instruct and guide those we love. Memory can be as selective and precise in recalling everything (what is it about those people who can answer all the questions on *Jeopardy*?), as it can be in stamping out conscious recollection of painful episodes in our lives we do not want to remember.

Out of memory springs meaning. The 'why' of what you do with your life. Why your educational choices, your career direction, why the spouse you married, the home you built. And at the end of the day, memory will provide the assessment of for what your life stood. Did you beat the odds, and live a life of significance? Did your passage through life touch, inspire, raise up, or comfort others? Did you make lasting contributions to your community, as well as to those whom you employed or with whom you worked?

As we have seen, in the traditional estate planning process, questions like this are not raised. In traditional planning money is the focus. Its goal is to just pass the money, without concern for or consideration of the values, work ethic, faith and other important characteristics that created the memories and shaped the meaning that defines our lives.

Traditional planning does not look back to what it took to accumulate your money. It only looks ahead to the 'iceberg tip' of taxes, fees and other obstacles that may stand in the way of getting more of your assets past the tax collector and to your inheritors.

"If you want to know your future," said Winston Churchill, *"look backwards first."* The Heritage Process looks back before it looks forward. It focuses on things that have deeper value to you and your family, rather than on the value of the things you have accumulated. As a result, the money becomes a tool again, instead of the focus for all you plan. Thus, the Process becomes a multi-generational planning and training platform designed to pass what you really value along with what you own.

The Heritage Process has equal merit for those who do not have families. Through it, the single person or married people without children can discover and articulate the values they hold dear, and design a plan that can enhance the lives of others, or underwrite the efforts of the charitable causes in which they believe.

If you believe that transmitting the values by which you lived to succeeding generations is an important, worthy goal, then ask yourself a question which traditional planning does not address:

"How do you pass on that which has brought you happiness and success?"

As you read about Guided Discovery and walked through the creation of your Vision Statement earlier in this book, you saw how the Process redefines the traditional view of wealth to include not only money and assets, but also the values, virtues and ethics that make life meaningful and fulfilling. You had the opportunity to reflect on and share the story behind your own accumulation of wealth. And you saw how through the process of ordering (or ranking) your financial objectives in line with your values, you could create a plan of great purpose and lasting significance.

Is The Heritage Process for you and your family? Ultimately, a person commits to the Process in order to achieve true significance. Not for fame, or lasting glory, but to validate the ethics, virtues and values by which they lived, and to participate in building a living plan that will help transmit those values to generations of their descendants.

In an earlier chapter, we asked you to imagine yourself seated at a great table in an enormous vaulted hall. To your left, we said you should envision all of the generations of your family who came before you. Hundreds of them, seated at the table, stretching as far as your eyes can see in that direction. Some in simple wool jackets, some in frontier calico, others in colonial lace. The heroes, the sinners, the providers, the builders, the scoundrels and the solid, common working folk who are your ancestors. The kinds of ancestors we all share. We asked you to imagine this scene when we explained that the values you received from them are the greatest inheritance you could ever possess.

You have walked through The Heritage Process in the pages of this book.

You have seen how the values you cherish can be molded into a vision and a plan for the benefit of your children, and theirs, for generations.

We would like to leave you with one more image as we close.

You are still seated at that enormous table, with your ancestors lined up on your left, chatting and eating and laughing and visiting.

Now, look to your right. As you peer down the length of the table to a point far, far off in the distance, to a place where a few rays of sunshine are just breaking through a wisp of clouds, imagine this: on your immediate right sit your children. Next to them sit their children, and then your great-grandchildren, great-great grandchildren, and generations of their grandchildren. Dozens of generations to come.

Unlike the ancestors to your left, who lived their lives, each in different measure, and who now talk and laugh of times gone by, the heirs seated to your right are quiet. Each sits expectantly. Hope and anticipation fill their eyes. Each holds an empty glass in his or her hand. Your great task is to fill that glass to the brim. Fill it with memory and meaning, with values that encourage, uplift and motivate. Fill it with faith, honor, respect, and love. Fill it with your story.

When you leave a legacy that is built on values, your descendants will know your story. They will remember your name. And they will honor your memory.

Appendices

Appendix 1

A Brief History of Estate Planning

"The mouth of a perfectly contented man is filled with pure waters."
With those words, the priest raised a jug of filtered water to the cloudless desert sky, then poured it out on top of the simple clay coffin. The water streamed across the terra-cotta lid, covered with a painted likeness of the coffin's occupant. Uah, sub-administrator in the corps of Sepdu, lord of the East, was ready for his final journey.

In ancient Egypt, the funeral of a government worker followed both law and custom, and the ceremonial pouring of clean water marked the close of the ritual. As soon as Uah's coffin was wedged into a small, nondescript tomb near the center of a vast complex of mud brick niches and burial vaults, his family gathered around a wooden table for the reading of his will.

The year was 1797 BC–over three thousand eight hundred years ago. In Uah's day, Egypt was tightly managed by a complex warren of civil law–much of it designed to protect private property. Estate planning customs and law had been around for many hundreds of years. When the priest read from the papyri will, he followed law that was already ancient when the first pyramids were built. Uah's assets were listed (except for his slaves–they were simply referred to as 'those who live upon my land'), provisions made for his first and second wives, and agreements reached by his four children prior to his death were made a matter of public record. Finally, a certified copy of the will was signed by the priest, who would see that it was filed in the temple in accordance with Pharaoh's estate law decrees.

Historians agree that the story of mankind's social ascent from primitive savagery to civil (political) society is largely the story of private property; in particular, how that property was acquired, developed, and passed on to the next generation.

In early cultures, land was held in common, as a group or clan. Land that was productive for food and easy to defend was a precious commodity. So precious that the world's first armies evolved to protect property, not to spread political or religious systems. And, as the land they defended remained under the control of one clan for generations, the practice of doling out a small parcel to individuals within the group developed. Having fought–and sometimes died–for that land, the sense of personal ownership became a powerful cultural force.* As social organization grew more complex, and populations grew, it only made sense that parents pass along their hard-won ground to their children. In a very real way, the absolute necessity for generally accepted rules of estate planning would become the catalyst for the emergence of civilization.

Over centuries, the crude wood and stone enclosures that protected clan groups of several dozen people grew into walled villages with hundreds of people, and the need to safeguard the inheritance of private property became increasingly important.

By the time Uah was being laid to rest in the Valley of the Nile, the people of ancient Mesopotamia were already living under the rule of the legal Code of

---

*Interestingly, the evolution of the idea of private property, and the right of inheritance existed in virtually every culture around the world thousands of years ago. Historian Louis H. Morgan points out that one enduring myth about Native Americans is that they had no private property, or only held land for the whole tribe. In fact, many tribes practiced individual ownership of property, and their laws for family succession and rules for selling lands were every bit as formal as those in Uah's Egypt.

King Hammurabi. Many of the Code's two hundred eighty-two laws dealt with economic issues, including estate planning. That is a focus that has remained steady across millennia: in a recent survey of international legal systems done by the University of Chicago, it was reported that over seventy-five percent of the laws on the books of any given nation dealt with property issues of one kind or another. King Hammurabi was truly ahead of his time.

For the classical Greeks, the concepts of the rule of law, and equality before the law, were based entirely on the primacy of protection of private property. Greek philosophers taught that private property was the well-spring from which all civilization developed, since by it man improved the soil, which provided for his family and strengthened his community.

(This is by no means a primitive or forgotten concept. Economist Murray N. Rothbard is in the mainstream of contemporary thinking when he says that, "all human rights are property rights." There can be no freedom of the press unless individuals are free to own printing presses, paper and ink. No freedom of speech unless an individual can own a hall or a radio station and invite anyone to speak on any topic. No freedom of religion unless individuals can build houses of worship. And all of these freedoms stem from the right to own and pass on property.)

Private property, and its transmission from generation to generation, was a deeply religious and cultural matter for the Greeks. They are credited as the first people to mark the boundaries of their property, which they did with small statues of household gods. The markers were a physical reflection of the family's daily prayer ritual. When a Greek asked a god to bless his land, he wanted the deity to know exactly where his land was!

The Romans took a much more practical approach to property and estate planning. Under *Lex Romana*, property rights were legal, secular matters, not religious, as they had been under the Egyptians and Greeks. When Rome imposed order upon its far-flung empire, it was done with laws covering property and commerce as much as it was by the soldiers of their Legions.

Roman law covered all aspects of contracts, mortgages, credit and banking transactions, torts, fraud, insurance—even corporations and partnerships. And whatever else the conquered peoples of Europe and North Africa didn't like about their Roman masters, they knew a good thing when they saw it, and quickly adopted Roman law for their own purposes. In ancient Britain, for example, land had been held in common by tribes until the Roman conquest. After that, a Briton who became a Roman citizen acquired the right to private property, which under Roman law, was granted in perpetuity. The perpetual right to ownership was taken seriously; two thousand years after the Roman conquest, there are hundreds of British landholders who can trace their ownership directly back to land grants and purchase contracts made during the Roman occupation.

With the collapse of Rome in the fifth century AD, the empire fragmented into hundreds of small kingdoms and principalities. In recent years, some historians have changed their minds about the commonly held view that this period should be called the 'Dark Ages', in part because from the fall of Rome to the blossoming of the Renaissance nine hundred years later, there continued to be a steady progression of innovative ideas and revisions in the law as it related to property. The end of the Empire did not mean everything Roman vanished from the face of the earth. Roman law remained the foundation of real estate and commercial transactions for over one thousand years.

In medieval times, one Roman estate planning tradition took root more than any other. That was the concept of primogeniture, which could be summed up in five words: *the eldest son shall inherit.* Before there were wills, property passed down by "Canons of Descent" which promoted the ownership of the oldest son. Males were preferred over females and older children were preferred over younger children. Primogeniture was the norm throughout most of Western Europe, and eventually became part of English common law. It was a primary impetus for exploration and conquest (as second and third born sons struck out for the New World because they'd never inherit the family lands), and even for the creation of the first tax loopholes.

(As bad as primogeniture was, other cultures had some estate and inheritance situations that were worse. In medieval Japan, Samurai warriors who committed ritual suicide seldom did it to 'save face'. Usually it was for a much more practical reason: should they be executed for any reason, the law provided that their lands and possessions went to their master, they could not be passed on to their heirs. If they committed suicide after a death sentence was pronounced, however, their family was allowed to inherit the warrior's estate.)

Before the sixteenth century it was extremely difficult to bequeath land. In medieval Europe, estates were not thought of as relationships between people, as they are today, but as actual things in themselves. That meant the Crown was often in a position to sell an estate to the highest bidder, or give it to loyal followers. So a legal loophole was exploited by landowners by which the land was conveyed during the holder's lifetime to trustees *"to hold to the use of the owner's will."* The document instructing the trustees was known as his "Will".

Henry VIII, whose appetite for wives and fine food was exceeded only by his desire to acquire property and conduct war, wasn't about to allow the lawyers of the day to outmaneuver his tax code. As a way of ensuring a steady stream or revenue to his coffers, he strong-armed Parliament into the passage of the Statute of Uses, which closed the tax avoidance loopholes.

Then in 1540, Henry supported the passage of the Statute of Wills, which made the bequeathing of land legal. Landowners could divide it among their heirs, give it to charity, even disinherit their children altogether if they wished—as long as the Crown received its inheritance tax. Other property (money, furniture, tools, crops, leases, etc.) was transferable by means of a "Testament," and after 1540 the two documents were combined into one. Any male over the age of fourteen, or female over the age of twelve (as long as she wasn't married—only a husband could approve of a wife's will) could make a valid will that planned for the passing of his or her estate.

The Statute of Wills governed estate planning in England—and soon most of Europe—until 1837. In fact, parts of the original Statute were still in use in Scotland until 1926. (In particular the prohibition against prisoners, lunatics or traitors being able to leave valid wills.)

Primogeniture, and the entire body of English Common law, accompanied the first settlers to the shores of America. But in the colonies, inheritance laws, like many European traditions, soon fell by the wayside. America had vast expanses of land that anyone could lay claim to (particularly as the native tribes were pushed further east and south), and as for the importance of family connections, the custom in colonial America was that if a man didn't venture his history, you didn't ask. The old rules of class-conscious medieval Europe didn't work in a place where a man could prosper through his own hard work and enterprise—no matter who his parents had been.

One of the differences between the American colonies and, say, the one-time penal colony of Australia was that America was settled by such a wide variety of peoples; in the pubs of Boston and Philadelphia, indentured servants and debtors rubbed shoulders with the second and third sons of landed gentry who had been excluded from significant inheritances by old world custom.

America offered a level playing field to all who wished to work and dream and sacrifice. In itself, this was a revolutionary condition. No society in history since the earliest hunter-gatherers had done so.

Primogeniture did prevail for some time in the southern colonies. With their large plantations, and slave-dependent economy, southern landowners struggled to retain the trappings of the English upper class. In the middle and northern colonies, however, the reality of hard-scrabble life on the rugged frontier brought huge changes in the established social structure.

As Governor Talcott of Connecticut said in 1699, "Much of our land remains unsubdued, and will remain so without the assistance of younger sons, which in reason can't be expected if they will have no part of the inheritance." So, a 'multigeniture' system quickly became the norm in the northern and middle colonies.

Thomas Jefferson believed that to own land and to make it productive was the birthright of every American. He also had his own strong feelings about traditional estate planning of the time that favored giving the eldest son a "double-portion" of the estate. "If he could eat twice as much or do double the work," it might be evidence of his right to a double portion of the estate. However, to Jefferson, the eldest son was "on a par in his powers and his wants" with his siblings, and so he concluded that equal inheritance was the preferable system.

In many ways the history of estate planning has been the history of taxation. That has been the case in the United States since the first federal estate tax was passed in 1797. From that day to ours, estate taxes have been applied, then rescinded, and applied again, as regularly as the changing tides. Funding wars, social programs, highway programs–the need for a constant flow (some would say torrent) of monies into the federal treasury has never declined. Estate taxation has always been an apple literally waiting to drop into the tax collector's outstretched hand.

In American history, the imposition of new estate taxes have often coincided with efforts to improve the national balance sheet in a time of military or social crisis. In 1797, when a blockade by the French navy threatened to wipe out trans-Atlantic trade, Congress passed the Stamp Act, which required citizens to purchase federal stamps on wills and other inheritance documents. This first estate tax raised funds to re-build the navy, and was repealed in 1802.

The first direct tax on inheritances came during the Civil War, with the passage of the Revenue Act of 1862. Blood relatives–other than spouses– receiving inheritances of more than $1,000 were required to pay a three-fourths of one percent tax. (It rose to five percent on gifts to more distant relatives or strangers.) In 1864, the top rate was raised to six percent. This tax was repealed in 1870.

The U.S. went to war again in 1898 war after the sinking of the battleship *Maine* in Cuba. To fund this war, Congress passed the War Revenue Act of 1898, which imposed taxes on both estates *and* gifts. Rates rose (after an exemption of $10,000) from three-fourths of one percent up to fifteen percent on estates over $1 million. Like its predecessors, this tax had a relatively short life, and was repealed in 1902.

Congress passed the Revenue Act of 1916 as America prepared to enter World War I. It levied taxes of from one percent after a $50,000 exemption– up to ten percent for estates valued at over $5 million. In 1917, the top rate was increased to twenty-five percent on estates above $10 million. Then in 1926, the estate tax was reduced, but, by this time, the notion of government ever turning its back on the estate tax gift horse looked increasingly unlikely.

Franklin Roosevelt turned to the estate tax to help fund New Deal programs. In 1932, the gift tax that had been abolished in 1924, was reinstated, and in 1934, the estate tax was increased to sixty percent for estates greater than $10 million. Unlike the repeals following other wars, the estate tax was not abolished after World War II. It was then, and remains today, a small part of overall federal revenues—about one and one-half percent, but in the days of trillion-dollar budgets, it still has an impact.

For most of the last five hundred years, people have looked at the estate planning process primarily from a tax perspective. The quest to minimize what one poet called 'a man's final and most humiliating tithe,' has dominated the process for so long, and with such complete effect, that for many it is hard to conceive of a world without a death tax.

But that day could come, and soon. The estate tax could finally be on the way to permanent extinction. Legislation passed in 2001 calls for its abolishment in 2010. (You may, however, want to leave the champagne cork in the bottle: should Congress not approve the hammering of the final nail in the coffin before then, estate and generation skipping taxes will be reinstated in 2011, in their pristine 2001 form.)

Presently, the reality of the estate tax is still the eight hundred pound gorilla of the financial planning process. The response by financial and legal advisors to the last grab of the tax collector's hand into their client's pockets as the coffin lid is being closed has been to develop a wide array of products and strategies to keep the pain of the 'last' tax bite to a minimum. And they've done a very good job providing that protection. Yet, by making the main focus of the estate planning process minimization of taxes, traditional advisors may have helped open a Pandora's box. These unanticipated problems have, over the years, destroyed more families, and more fortunes, than any estate tax in history.

Those problems, and their solutions, are the focus of this book. They can be traced back thousands of years, to the first primitive landholder who ever fought off marauding neighbors so that he could lay claim to a small patch of fertile, defendable land. Who would inherit the land when he no longer had the strength to lead the clan? What would his children, and their children, make of the gift he would pass to them? Would they really ever understand the sacrifice that went into making the land valuable? Would they instruct their own children the way he had taught them? And, of course, would they know how to pay proper tribute of grain and fresh meat to the elders who had the power of life and death over everyone in the village?

Thousands of years ago, those questions haunted a father who owned property, and who understood his mortality. They are not all that different than the questions which dominate our planning practices today–especially the part about paying tribute.

Why we are still focusing on those questions, *to the exclusion of questions that matter even more* if we want to create a plan–a legacy–that will help generations of our family thrive, is an important question. With the development of The Heritage Process, it is a question that can finally be answered.

Appendix II

Relevant Terms

The Heritage Process: A guided discovery process for individuals and families who desire to pass both their moral and financial net worth (their values and their valuables) to the people they love and the causes they care about. The Heritage Process enhances traditional financial and estate planning. The Process is guided by professional advisors certified to work with individuals and families, and, when appropriate, with their existing advisors. The goal of The Heritage Process is the development and implementation of a unique, multi-disciplinary plan to support family unity, individual achievement and community involvement across generations. These plans rest on a foundation of values that are unique to the individuals and families involved.

In these plans, money is regarded as a tool to support the real inheritance; the values, ethics and beliefs that you pass on to your inheritors.

Guided Discovery: A process of learning during which you are guided by your Heritage Advisor to learn from your own experiences.

Its objective is to assist you to learn from your own experiences. It helps identify and clarify the values that you and your family hold dear and desire to pass on to future generations.

Vision Statement: A meaningful and compelling statement of your story and values, coupled with your vision for sharing those values with future generations. Your Vision Statement is as unique as your family, and it is intended to inspire and guide for generations. It describes the responsibilities of the family as a group, and also of each individual within it in the pursuit of family unity and the support of shared values. It also details the expectation that each member of the family will strive to leave their own legacy of both 'self and wealth' to future generations of the family, and to the society in which they live.

Family Retreat: A special family event that provides the opportunity to implement a family structure, broaden the family leadership base, strengthen family commitments and pass on family values. At the first retreat, the family is introduced to Guided Discovery exercises for the children, and parents tell their story, including how they accumulated their wealth. The family is introduced to the Vision Statement, they may assess the family's 'human capital,' and they will formally organize the Family Council. Ongoing family retreat's, where fun mixes with family business and education, are held at least annually.

Family Council: A family forum where all family members participate in activities, events and experiences to promote family unity, family values and family traditions. The Family Council draws upon the family's unique human capital, made up of the collective knowledge, talents, experience, values, skills, judgment and potential of each family member.

Appendix III

Enhancing Your Planning
with The Heritage Process

(See overleaf)

Enhancing Your Planning *with the* Heritage Process

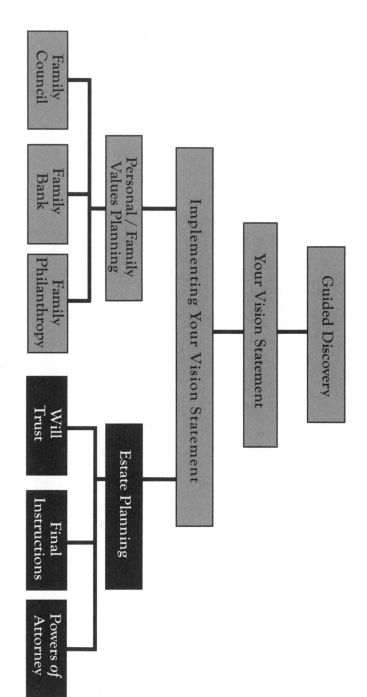

- Guided Discovery
- Your Vision Statement
- Implementing Your Vision Statement
  - Personal / Family Values Planning
    - Family Council
    - Family Bank
    - Family Philanthropy
  - Estate Planning
    - Will Trust
    - Final Instructions
    - Powers of Attorney

Appendix IV

Expanded Biographies
for
Perry Cochell and Rod Zeeb

PERRY L. COCHELL is the Associate Regional Director/Senior Endowment Counsel for the Boy Scouts of America, Western Region. Perry supports council professionals and volunteers in the development and implementation of endowment programs. He serves as the technical expert in all areas of tax for current and deferred gifts to councils.

Perry earned his Doctorate of Jurisprudence from Willamette University, College of Law in Oregon. He completed his graduate studies at Brigham Young University in Provo, Utah, and earned a Bachelor of Arts degree from Arizona State University in Tempe, Arizona.

Perry is a member of the American Bar Association (ABA) and is a Committee member of the ABA's section on Taxation, and Property, Probate and Trust Law. He is a Committee member of the Emotional and Psychological Issues in Estate Planning of the Real Property, Probate and Trust Law Section of the ABA. Perry also has served on various ABA's Task

Forces for Charitable Giving. As a member of the Idaho State Bar Association (ISB), Perry has also been the chairman of the Legislative Committee of the (ISB) Tax Section as well as past chairman of the Current Affairs Committee of the ISB Tax Section.

Perry is a Certified Wealth Consultant with The Heritage Institute.

Perry is co-founder, faculty chair and senior faculty instructor for The Heritage Institute, which provides consulting, training and tools to professional advisors and to individuals and families who want to pass both their values and their valuables to future generations. As Faculty Chair, Perry has created The Heritage Institute's Family Portfolio, Process Portfolio, Mentor Manual, and the curriculum for the Institute's *Counseling the Affluent* course and *Advanced Practice Academies*.

Perry is an Eagle Scout, and has been a Scoutmaster, and loves to fish. Perry and his wife, Karen, have three daughters and two sons. They live in Mesa, Arizona.

RODNEY C. ZEEB graduated Summa Cum Laude from Willamette College of Law in 1986, where he was Editor-in-Chief of the Willamette Law Review (1985-86). Rod earned a Bachelor of Science degree in economics from Willamette University in 1977. Rod's law practice encompassed business and real estate transactions, financial, estate and retirement planning, estate administration and probate, and related tax issues.

Rod is a member of the Oregon State Bar, and of OSB's Business Law, Estate Planning, Real Property & Land Use sections. He is also a member of the National Committee on Planned Giving and the Northwest Planned Giving Roundtable. Rod was active in the American Bar Association for many years, and was a member of the ABA's Business Law, Real Property, Probate and Trust sections.

He is certified as an Advanced Wealth-Strategist Planner by The Esperti Peterson Institute for Global Wealth Strategies Planning, and as a Certified Wealth Consultant by The Heritage Institute.

Rod is co-founder, President, CEO and senior faculty instructor for The Heritage Institute, which provides consulting, training and tools to professional advisors and to individuals and families who want to pass both their values and their valuables to future generations. Rod's publications include *Giving: Philanthropy for Everyone,* Quantum Press, LLC (2003) (contributing author); "Abolishing Tort Immunities in Oregon: Two Steps Forward, One Sidestep," 21 Willamette L. Rev. 349 (1985) (co-author); and "Witters v. Commission for the Blind: An Individual's Use of State Aid Creates a Violation of the Establishment Clause," 21 Willamette L. Rev. 954 (1985).

Rod is sought after as a speaker on legacy, charitable, and estate planning topics. He has presented seminars sponsored by numerous charities such as American Cancer Society, Northwest Medical Teams, American Heart Association, Boy Scouts of America, and the United Way.

Rod is active in many church, charitable, and community organizations. He enjoys golf, skiing, and other activities with his children, Christina and Ryan, Ryan's wife Kristin and his granddaughter Alexa.

Appendix V

A Note on Research and Methodology

In the years they have spent developing and refining The Heritage Process, Perry Cochell and Rod Zeeb have relied upon the latest academic studies and research, as well as their own experience and that of other advisors from many disciplines.

They have conducted extensive research in these areas:

1. The history of wealth.

2. The history of inheritance.

3. The psychological effects of wealth on heirs. (Affluenza.)

4. Values and how they are derived.

5. Patterns, behaviors and attitudes used by individuals who accumulate wealth.

6. The methodologies of adult learning.

7. Psychological relationships between and among parents and their adult children.

8. How those who achieved wealth relate to their money.

9. Effects of charitable giving as a philanthropic tool to teach beneficiaries about the needs of others.

10. The role and expectations of professionals in facilitating family communication, unity, organization/structure and in passing leadership to the next generation.

11. The role that money plays in destroying familial relationships.

12. Inter-disciplinary studies in the fields of estate, financial and values planning; team planning with families of wealth.

Appendix VI

Requirements for Earning
a Certified Wealth Consultant
Designation

The Heritage Institute, established for the purpose of providing support and advanced training for advisors, requires that its members exhibit and maintain the highest ethical and professionals standards. Only highly experienced and qualified professional are invited to join the Institute. Some of its members go on to earn the designation: Certified Wealth Consultant (CWC).

In order for the Heritage Institute to certify a Member as a CWC they must:

• Successfully complete the Counseling the Affluent course

• Establish and maintain a mentor relationship with a senior Member

• Themselves mentor a provisional Member

199

- Complete a demanding curriculum of reading and course work that includes
    - seven books for the initial course
    - successful completion of the *Fast Start Forum* (which includes six more books)
    - a personal sabbatical
    - completion of their own Heritage Process plan (for themselves and their family)
    - six *Advanced Practice Academies* (at least once per year in person)
    - ongoing, active participation in The Heritage Institute

- Complete at least two Heritage Process cases (including at least one Family Retreat)

In addition, in order to annually renew their professional designation, they must:

- Maintain good standing in their profession

- Continue to comply with THI's Code of Conduct and Ethics

- Attend at least one *Advanced Practice Academy* in person, per year

- Actively participate with other members in online forums on The Heritage Process

- Serve on one of the Institute's boards, councils or committees

Anyone receiving the Certified Wealth Consultant™ designation has been thoroughly trained in The Heritage Process and is qualified to lead clients in all phases of the Process, including Guided Discovery, Vision Statement, Vision Implementation, and Family Retreats.

Chapter Notes

CHAPTER TWO

1 "Information Overload Statistics," Humboldt State University California Library, 2004

CHAPTER THREE

1 "Millionaires and the Millennium: New Estimates of the Forthcoming Wealth Transfer and the Prospects for a Golden Age of Philanthropy," by the Social Welfare Research Institute at Boston College, 1999

2 "The Greatest Century That Ever Was," Cato Institute for Policy Analysis, 1999

3 *The Autobiography of Andrew Carnegie*, by Andrew Carnegie, Northeastern University Press, 1986

4 William K Vanderbilt quote, page 39
The Vanderbilts, by Jerry E. Patterson, Harry Abrams, New York, 1989

CHAPTER FOUR

1   *A Time to Search*, by Joe Boot, 2002, Kingsway Press, East Sussex, England

2   *The Golden Ghetto*, by Jessie O'Neil, 1997, The Affluenza Project

CHAPTER SIX

1   William Sanford, Phd & Carl Green, Phd, *American Government*, AMSCO Publications, 1997

2   United States Department of Agriculture, 2004
    http://www.srs.fs.usda.gov/sustain/data/authors/glossary.htm

CHAPTER SEVEN

1   CNN Money July 28, 2005

CHAPTER EIGHT

1   Merrill Lynch and Capgemini "2004 World Wealth Report"

CHAPTER NINE

1   *Dragons of Eden, Speculations on the Evolution of Human Intelligence*, by Carl Sagan, Ballantine Publishing, 1977

CHAPTER TEN

1   "Earthly Debts, Heavenly Debts," Joseph B. Wirthlin, Ensign, May 2004

CHAPTER ELEVEN

1   National Tax Limitation Foundation, Roseville, CA

2   *Stengel: His Life and Times,* by Robert W. Creamer, Simon & Schuster, 1984

CHAPTER TWELVE

1   Coca-Cola Chairman Roberto C. Goizueta, address to shareholders, 1991

CHAPTER 14

1   Giving USA Foundation , "Giving USA 2004"

2. J.P. Morgan Private Bank, "World Philanthropy," 2004

3   John J. Havens & Paul G. Schervish, "Why the $41 Trillion Wealth Transfer Estimate is Still Valid, A Review of Challenges and Questions," 2003

4   Ernest Becker, *The Denial of Death*, Simon & Schuster, 1973

5   Peter F. Drucker, *Innovation & Entrepreneurship*, Harper, 1985

CHAPTER FIFTEEN

1   The U.S. Trust Annual Survey of Affluent Americans, "What the Wealthy Think," 2003

CHAPTER SEVENTEEN

1   Fortune Magazine, September 29, 1997

Selected Bibliography

The expanded and annotated bibliography can
be accessed online at: www.beatingthemidascurse.com

Allen-Burley, Madelyn. *Listening.* New York, NY: John Wiley & Sons, Inc., 1995.

Allport, Gordon, W.P.E. Vernon and Garnder Lindzey. *Study of Values.* Boston: Houghton, Mifflin, 1960.

Anderson, J.R. *Learning and Memory.* New York: Wiley, 1995.

Atkinson, J.W. and D. Birch. *Introduction to Motivation* (2nd ed.). New York: Wiley, Van Nostrand, 1978.

Atkinson, R.K., S.J. Derry, A. Renkl and D. Worham. *Learning from examples: instructional principles from the worked examples research.* Review of Educational Research, 70, 181-214 (2000).

Avery, Robert B. and Michael S. Rendall. *Estimating the size and distribution of baby boomers' prospective inheritances.* Cornell University for Presentation at the Philanthropy Roundtable, (Nov. 11, 1993).

Avery, Robert B. and Michael S. Rendall. *Inheritance and wealth.* Cornell University For Presentation at the Philanthropy Roundtable, (Nov. 11,1993). "The Cornell Study."

Bernstein, William J. *The Birth of Plenty.* New York, NY: McGraw-Hill Publishing, 2004.

Bower, G.H. *The Nature of Emotion.* New York: Oxford University Press, 1994. Some relations between emotions and memory. In P. Ekman and R.J. Davidson (Eds.).

Boyack, Merrilee Brown. *The Parenting Breakthrough.* Salt Lake City, UT: Deseret Book Company, 2005.

Boyatzis, Richard E., Angela J. Murphy and Jane V. Wheeler. *Philosophy as a missing link between values and behavior.* Psychological Reports, 86, 47-64 (2000).

Bradley, Susan and Mary Martin. *Sudden Money.* New York, NY: John Wiley & Sons Inc., 2002.

Bradshaw, John. *The Family.* Deerfield Beach, Florida: Health Communications, Inc, 1998.

Bragstad, B.J. and S.M. Stumpf. *A Guidebook for Teaching Study Skills and Motivation.* Boston: Allyn & Bacon, 1982.

Brancaccio, David. *Squandering Aimlessly.* New York, NY: Simon & Schuster, 2000.

Bransford, J.D., J. J. Franks, N.J. Vye and R.D. Sherwood. *Similarity and Analogical Reasoning.* Cambridge, England: Cambridge University Press, 1989, pp. 470-497. New approaches to instruction: because wisdom can't be told. In S. Vosniadou & A. Ortony (Eds.).

Brickman, S., R.B. Miller and T.D. Roedel. *Goal valuing and future consequences as predictors of cognitive engagement.* Paper presented at the annual meeting of the American Educational Research Association, Chicago (March 1997).

Brill, Marla. *Windfall.* Indianapolis, IN: ALPHA, 2002.

Brinkman, Rick and Rick Kirschner. *Dealing with Relatives.* New York, NY: McGraw-Hill, 2003.

Broadbent, D.E. *Perception and Communication.* London: Pergamon Press, 1958.

Brooks, Andree Aelion. *Children of Fast-Track Parents.* New York, NY: Penguin Group, 1989.

Brooks, David. *Bobos In Paradise.* New York, NY: Simon & Schuster, 2000.

Brophy, J.E. and J. Alleman. *Advances in Research on Teaching.* Greenwich, CT: JAI Press, 1992.

Bruner, J.S. *The act of discovery.* Harvard Educational Review, 31, 21-32 (1961).

Burley-Allen, Madelyn. *Listening: The Forgotten Skill.* Canada: John Wiley & Sons, Inc., 1995.

Butler, D.L. and P.H. Winne. *Feedback and self-regulated learning: a theoretical synthesis.* Review of Educational Research, 65, 245-281 (1995).

B.Z. Posner and W.H. Schmidt. *Values congruence and differences between and interplay of personal and organizational value systems.* Journal of Business Ethics, 12, 171-177 (1993).

Callahan, Sidney Cornelia. *Parents Forever.* New York: Crossroads
     Publishing Co., 1992.

Card, Emily W. and Adam L. Miller. *Managing Your Inheritance.* New York:
     Times Books, 1996.

Carroll, Lenedra J. *The Architecture of All Abundance.* Novato, CA: New
     World Library, 2001.

Christiansen, Tim and Sharon A. DeVaney. *Antecedents of trust
     and commitment in the financial planner-client relationship.*
     Association for Financial Counseling and Planning Education,
     (1998).

Ciaramicoli, Arthur and Katherine Ketcham. *The Power of Empathy.* New
     York: Dutton, 2000.

Cleary, Thomas. *The Art of Wealth.* Deerfield Beach, FL: Health
     Communications, 1998.

Coles, Robert. *Privileged Ones.* Boston: Little, Brown & Company, 1977.

Collier, Charles W. *Wealth in Families.* Published by Harvard University,
     2002.

Communicating more effectively with older clients. Trusts & Estates,
     p. 58 (April 2000).

Controlling behavior by controlling the inheritance. Probate & Property,
     p. 6 (Sept/Oct)

Crawford, Tad. *The Secret Life of Money.* New York: G.P. Putnam's Sons, 1994.

Cutler, Neal E. *Advising Mature Clients.* New York: John Wiley & Sons Inc.,
     2002.

D'Souza, Dinesh. *The Virtue of Prosperity.* New York: NY: TouchStone, 2000.

Dalphonse, Sherri. *Love and money.* Washington, 48 (Feb 2000).

Damon, William. *The Moral Child.* New York: The Free Press, 1988.

Davis, Ken and Tom Taylor. *Kids and Cash.* La Jolla, CA: Oak Tree Publications, Inc., 1979.

DeGraaf, John, David Wann and Thomas H. Naylor. *Affluenza.* San Francisco, CA: Berrett-Koehler Publishers, Inc., 2001.

Dominguez, Joe and Vicki Robin. *Your Money or Your Life.* New York: Penguin, 1992, xx.

Domini, Amy L., Dennis Pearne and Sharon L. Rich. *The Challenges of Wealth.* Homewood, IL: Dow Jones-Irwin, 1998.

DuFour, Richard and Robert Eaker. *Professional Learning Communities at Work.* Bloomington, IN: National Educational Service, 1998.

Easterbrook, Gregg. *The Progress Paradox.* New York: Random House Trade Paperbacks, 2004.

Edelman, Ric. *Ordinary People, Extraordinary Wealth.* New York, NY: HarperCollins, 2000.

Erikson, Joan M. *The Life Cycle Completed.* New York, NY: W.W. Norton & Company, 1997.

Eyre, Linda & Richard. *Teaching Your Children Values.* New York, NY: Fireside, 1993.

Fish, Barry, Les Kotzer. *The Family Fight.* Washington D.C.: Continental Atlantic Publications Inc., 2002.

Fisher, Marc. *Naming your price-many Americans find that the money they desire is never quite enough.* Washington Post, C1 (June 30, 1997).

Ford, M.E. *Motivating Humans.* Newbury Park, CA: Sage, 1992.

Forward, Susan, and Craig Buck. *Toxic Parents.* New York: Bantam Books, 1989.

Frank, Robert. *Luxury Fever.* New York, NY: The Free Press, 1999.

Gagnier, Regenia. *The Insatiability of Human Wants.* Chicago, IL: The University of Chicago Press, 2000.

Gallo, Eileen and John Gallo. *Silver Spoon Kids.* New York, NY: Contemporary Books, 2002.

Gardner, Howard. *Changing Minds.* Boston, MA: Harvard Business School Press, 2004.

Gates, William H., Sr., and Chuck Collins. *Wealth and Our Common Wealth.* Boston, MA:Beacon Press, 2002.

Gilbert, Roberta M. *Extraordinary Relationships.* New York: John Wiley, 1992.

Glaser, R. *Cognitive Functioning and Social Structure over the Life Course.* Norwood, NJ: Ablex, 1987.

Grant, James. *The Trouble with Prosperity.* New York: Times Books, 1996.

Gurney, Kathleen. *Knowing your money personality can help you find the right financial advisor for you.* Financial Psychology Corporation, (1999).

Gutherie, E.R. *The Psychology of Learning.* New York: Harper & Row, 1935.

Hall, J.F. *The Psychology of Learning.* Philadelphia: J.B. Lippincott, 1966.

Handy, Charles. *The Age of Paradox.* Boston, Massachusetts: Harvard Business School Press, 1994.

Hausner, Lee. *Children of Paradise.* Los Angeles, CA: Jeremy P. Tarcher, 1990.

Hayes, Christopher L. *What's your money personality?* Working Woman, 35 (Feb 1995).

Hetcher, Michael, Lynn Nadel, and Richard E. Michod, eds. *The Origin of Values.* New York: Aldinc dc Gruyter, 1993. p. 1-28.

Hoffman, M.L. *Moral Behavior and Development.* Hillsdale, NJ: Erlbaum, 1991.

Empathy, social cognition, and moral action. In W.M. Kurtines & J.L. Gewirtz (Eds.).

Hughes, James E., Jr. *Family Wealth.* Princeton Junction, NJ: NetWrx, Inc., 1997.

Interviewing the affluent: unpacking philanthropic values and motivations." 11th National Conference on Planned Giving, (Oct 9, 1998).

Jones, Laurie Beth. *The Path.* New York, NY: Tyndale House Publishers, 1971.

Kinder, George. *The Seven Stages of Money Maturity.* New York, NY: Dell Publishing, 1997.

Kleberg, Sally S. *The Stewardship of Private Wealth.* NY: McGraw-Hill, 1997.

Klingelhofer, Edwin L. *Coping with Your Grown Children.* Clifton, NJ: Humana Press, 1989.

Kluckhohn, Florence and Fred Strodtbeck. *Variations in Value Orientations.* Evanston, IL: Row, Peterson & Co, 1961.

Kohn, Alfie. *Punished by Rewards.* New York: Houghton Mifflin Co., 1999.

Kotre, John PH.D. *Make it Count.* NY, NY: The Free Press, 1999.

Lave, J., and E. Wenger E. *Situated Learning.* Cambridge, England: Cambridge University Press, 1991.

Lennick, Doug and Fred Kiel. *Moral Intelligence.* Upper Saddle River, NJ: Wharton School Publishing, 2005.

Linder, Ray. *What Will I Do with My Money?* Chicago, IL: Northfield Publishing, 2000.

Link, E.G. and Peter Tedstrom. *Getting to the Heart of the Matter.* Franklin, Indiana: Professional Mentoring Program, 1999.

M. Rokeach, *The Nature of Human Values.* New York: Free Press, 1973.

Martin, V.L. and M. Pressley. *Elaborative-interrogation effects depend on the nature of the question.* Journal of Educational Psychology, 83, 113-119 (1991).

Massialas, B.G. and J. Zevin. *Teaching Creatively: Learning through Discovery.* Malabar, FL: Robert F. Krieger, 1983.

McAleese, Tama. *Money Power for Families.* Hawthorne, NJ: The Career Press, 1993.

McBride, Tracey. *Frugal Luxuries.* New York: Bantam Books, 1997.

McInerney, Francis and Sean White. *Future Wealth.* New York: St. Martin's Press, 2000.

Mellan, Olivia. *Money Harmony*. New York: Walker and Company, 1994.

Needleman, Jacob. *Money and the Meaning of Life*. New York: Doubleday, 1991.

Nemeth, Maria. *The Energy of Money*. New York: Ballantine Publishing Group, 1997.

Morris, P. *Adult Learning*. London: Wiley, 1977.

Nichols, Michael P. *The Lost Art of Listening*. New York, NY: The Guilford Press, 1995.

Olsen, Timothy. *The Teenage Investor*. NY: McGraw-Hill, 2003.

Patterson, Kerry, Joseph Grenny, Ron McMillian, and Al Switzler. *Crucial Conversations*. New York, NY. McGraw-Hill, 2002.

Pearl, Jayne A. *Kids and Money*. Princeton, NJ: Bloomberg Press, 1999.

Potter, Peter. *All About Money*. New Canaan, CT: William Mulvey, Inc., 1988.

Price, Deborah L. *Money Therapy*. Novato, CA: New World Library, 2000.

Prince, Russ Alan and Karen Maru File. *The Seven Faces of Philanthropy*. San Francisco, CA: Jossey-Bass Publishers, 1994.

Raising a responsible child of wealth. Trusts & Estates, p. 42 (June 2001).

Restraining on inheritance can accomplish a client's objectives. Estate Planning, p. 124 (March 2003).

Rosenberg, Claude Jr. *Wealthy and Wise*. Canada: Little, Brown & Company Limited, 1994.

Rottenberg, Dan. *The Inheritor's Handbook*. New York, NY: Fireside, 1999.

Russell, Bob. *Money.* Sisters, OR: Multnomah Books, 1977.

Schervish, P.G. *Philanthropy among the wealthy: empowerment, motivation, and strategy.* Paper presented on the Rocky Mountain Philanthropic Institute, Vail, CO, (July 1991).

Schwartz, Shalom H. *Universals in the content and structure of value: theoretical advances and empirical tests in 20 countries.* Advances in Experimental Social Psychology. NY: Academic Press, 5, 1-65 (1992).

Sedgwich, John. *Rich Kids.* New York: William Morrow, 1972.

Shore, Bill. *The Cathedral Within.* New York: Random House, 1999.

Solomon, Robert J. *When are unequal bequests to children equitable?* Estate Planning, 139 (March 2004).

Spence, Linda. *Legacy.* Athens, OH: Swallow Press, 1977.

Stanley, Thomas. *Marketing to the Affluent.* New York: McGraw-Hill, 1988.

Stanley, Thomas J. *The Millionaire Mind.* Kansas City, MO: Andrew McMeel Publishing, 2000.

Steiger, Heidi L. *Wealthy & Wise.* Hoboken, New Jersey: John Wiley & Sons, 2003.

Twist, Lynne. *The Soul of Money: Transforming.* New York: W.W. Norton & Company, 2003.

Vitt, Lois, Carol Anderson, Jamie Kent, Danna M. Lyter, Jurg K. Siegenthaler, and Jeremy Ward. *Personal finance and the rush to competence: financial literacy education in the U.S.* A Study Conducted by: The Institute of Socio-Financial Studies for the Fannie Mae Foundation, (2000).

Williams, Roy & Vic Preisser. *Philanthropy Heirs & Values.* Bandon, OR: Robert D. Reed Publishers, 2005.

Willis, Thayer Cheatham. *Navigating the Dark Side of Wealth.* Portland, OR: New Concord Press, 2003.

Wixon, Burton N. *Children of the Rich.* New York: Crown, 1973.

Woloshyn, V.E., M. Pressley and W. Schneider. *Elaborative-interrogation and prior knowledge effects on learning of facts.* Journal of Educational Psychology, 84, 115-124 (1992).

Wong, B.Y.L. *Self-questioning instructional research: a review.* Review of Educational Research, 55, 227-268 (1985).

Zelizer, Viviana A. *The Social Meaning of Money.* New York, NY: BasicBooks, 1994.

Zimmerman, Stuart and Jared Rosen. *Inner Security & Infinite Wealth.* NY: SelectBooks Inc., 2003.

The Contributing Authors

Each contributing author is a member of The Heritage Institute.

The Heritage Institute, LLC
Ryan Zeeb
Executive Director
1800 Blankenship Road, Suite 310
West Linn, OR 97068
(503) 655-3786
(877) 447-1659
www.theheritageinstitute.com

Michael Begin, CFP® and Daryl LePage, CFP®
Begin, LePage & Co., LLC
2080 Silas Deane Highway, Suite 304
Rocky Hill, CT 06067
860-257-8688
michael@beginlepage.com
daryl@beginlepage.com

Brian M. Bell, CWC
Mentor Chair for The Heritage Institute
1800 Blankenship Road, Suite 310
West Linn, OR 97068
503-655-3786
brian@theheritageinstitute.com

Paul Binnion, Senior Vice President
Liz Donaghy, William Hughes, Sean Kane, Harry Clark
Clark Capital Management Group, Inc.
1735 Market Street, 34th Floor
Philadelphia, PA 19103
215-569-2224
215-569-3639 (fax)
pbinnion@ccmg.com
www.ccmg.com

James H. Dean CLU, ChFC
Sagemark Consulting
555 White Plains Road, Suite 200
Tarrytown, NY 10591
914-333-7644
jdean@LNC.com
www.jamesdeanrescue.com

William M. Eck, CWC
Director of Wealth Management
Rocky Mountain Adventist Healthcare Foundation
7995 East Prentice Avenue, Suite 204
Greenwood Village, CO 80111

Tom Fowler
Fowler Financial
365 118th Avenue, Suite 200
Bellevue, WA 98005
425-453-1585
tom@fowlerfinancial.com

Louise Cole, Bill Cole, Tony DeGregorio, Phil Purpura
The Heritage Group of North America
250 Washington Street
P.O. Box 1450A
Toms River, NJ 08754
800-343-9448
info@thgona.com

Mark Johnson
913 W. River St., Ste. 400
Boise, ID 83702
800-605-6669
Mark.johnson@axa-advisors.com

Larry Knudsen
Financial Security Group
1001 4th Avenue, Suite 2800
Seattle, WA 98154
888-453-1020
Larry.kundsen@fsgllc.com

Janet Krakowiak
Wealth Counselors of New Mexico, LLC
HC 66 Box 79
Deming, New Mexico 88030
505-895-3316
jkr@starband.net

Connie Seay
CEMCO
2129 E. 23rd Street
Tulsa, OK 74114
918-747-7790
Qcon@aol.com

David W. Shepherd, ChFC, CFP®
Retirement Financial Services Inc.
6300 E. El Dorado Plaza, Suite A-200
Tucson, AZ 85715
520-325-1600
dave@retirementfinacial.com

Robert A. Strommen
Registered Representative, Tower Square Securities, Inc.
Strommen & Associates, Inc.
www.strommen.com
612-331-3805
Corporate Benefit Administrators, Inc.
www.cba401k.com
612-331-3736

Peter Toll
Ameriprise Financial
1800 Blankenship Road, Suite 300
West Linn, OR 97068
503-656-6612
Theodore.p.toll@ampf.com

Larry L. Van Oort
Family Legacy Planning Specialists ™
411 Clay Street
Cedar Falls, IA 50613
319-277-6040
private@lvanoort.com

NOTES

NOTES

NOTES

NOTES

NOTES

NOTES